THE ISLAND SERIES

CORSICA

THE ISLAND SERIES

CORSICA

by *IAN THOMPSON*

DAVID & CHARLES

NEWTON ABBOT

ISBN 0 7153 5329 2

Set in eleven on thirteen point Baskerville
and printed in Great Britain
by Clarke Doble & Brendon Limited Plymouth
for David & Charles (Publishers) Limited
South Devon House Newton Abbot Devon

To my parents

CONTENTS

ILLUSTRATIONS

ILLUSTRATIONS

Photographs other than those acknowledged are by the author. The jacket illustration of an aerial view of Bonifacio at the southern tip of Corsica is reproduced by courtesy of the French Government Tourist Office

MAPS

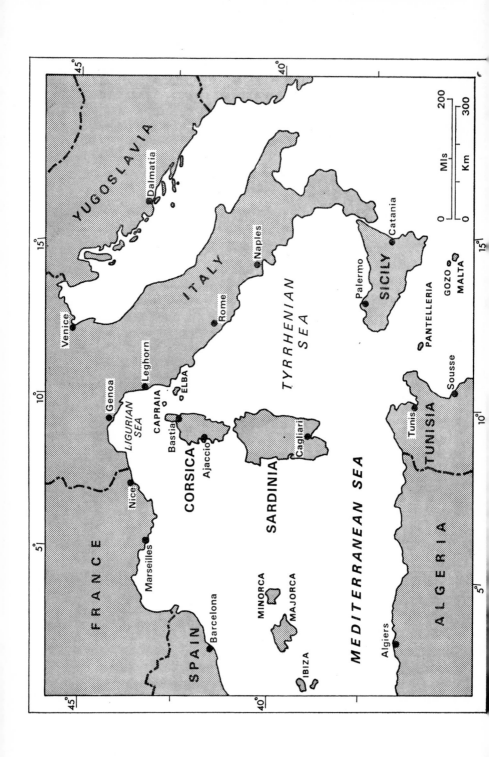

1   A MOUNTAIN IN THE SEA

To the romanticist, Corsica is a 'mountain in the sea', 'the scented isle' and the 'Ile de Beauté'. To the consultant of gazetteers, Corsica is an island in the western basin of the Mediterranean, physically detached from mainland France, but an integral part of the French nation. Somewhere between these extremes of the poetic and the banal is the real Corsica which this book seeks to introduce.

Corsica has a total land area of 8,722 square kilometers, roughly comparable to the area of Wales. The island extends 180 kilometres from the tip of Cap Corse to the Straits of Bonifacio, and the maximum distance between the eastern and western coasts is approximately 80 kilometres. These dimensions have little meaning in reality, for the contorted mountainous relief forces roads to detour as they seek easier gradients to passes, and distance 'as the crow flies' is something of an abstraction. The dimensions do, however, permit comparisons with the size of other Mediterranean islands, and in this context Corsica may be regarded as 'medium-sized'. It is much smaller than neighbouring Sardinia (24,089 square kilometers) and Sicily (25,708 square kilometres) but is greater in area than the largest of the Balearic Islands, Majorca (3,634 square kilometres) and much larger than all the remaining islands of the western Mediterranean.

Although politically part of France, the island is much closer geographically to Italy. A distance of only 12 kilometres separates Corsica from the Italian island of Sardinia, while in the north Bastia is only 82 kilometres from the Italian mainland. By contrast, the nearest point of mainland France is 160 kilometres distant. Corsica is a constituent of the triangle of land enclosing the

11

Tyrrhenian Sea, and the political attachment to France is an accident of history rather than a dictate of geography.

In proportion to the area, the population is very small and Corsica is one of the most sparsely populated islands in the whole Mediterranean. Some uncertainty surrounds the exact population total for the census data is notoriously inaccurate. The most reliable estimate places the permanent population of the island in 1970 as approximately 180,000. Since half of this population resides in the two principal towns of Bastia and Ajaccio it follows that rural population densities are extremely low, approximately 11 persons per square kilometre, and large sections of the island are practically uninhabited. In this, as in so many other respects, Corsica is the odd man out among Mediterranean islands, for Malta has an average population density of over 1,000 persons per square kilometre, Sicily 185, Sardinia 60, and the Balearic islands 90.

The title 'a mountain in the sea' which heads this chapter is extremely apt, for Corsica is the most mountainous island in the Mediterranean. Only Mount Etna, over 3,200m high in Sicily, exceeds Corsica's highest peak Monte Cinto, 2,710m, and no other island has such an unbroken mass of mountainous terrain unrelieved by extensive lowlands. The mountain backcloth and the marine setting provide the key to an understanding of human development on the island.

THE MOUNTAIN

To be strictly accurate, Corsica is not one mountain, but two. The island has been created by the fusion of two contrasted mountain systems. The whole of western and central Corsica, west of a line from St Florent and Corte to Solenzara, over two-thirds of the island, is composed of crystalline rocks, chiefly granite. These are the oldest rocks in Corsica and are a remnant of a former land mass, joined to the continent, which was up-lifted as a mountain range by earth movements some 250 million years ago. These mountains were gradually reduced by erosion to a plateau form which persisted until the next period of earth movements, some fifty million years ago, which created the great Alpine chains of Europe. In Corsica these movements lifted up the plateau *en masse*, imparting new vigour to the rivers, which carved out the present tormented relief. The uplift raised the crestline of the crystalline mountains within the range of glacial conditions during the Ice Age. The summits of the highest mountains bear the imprint of erosion by glaciers and even now are only free of snow for a short period each summer.

The result of this eventful geological history has been to stamp certain characteristics on the crystalline mountains which have deeply affected Corsican life. The mountains have the form of tilted blocks deeply gouged by powerful rivers aligned parallel to each other and flowing from the north-east to the south-west. The result is a herringbone pattern of relief in which the central crestline forms the island's spine, from which over twenty high parallel ridges diverge at regular intervals. The effect of this relief is to make central and western Corsica at once the most grandiose and spectacular part of the island and the most uncompromising environment for settlement and economic activity. Freedom of movement is greatly impeded. North-south access is reduced by the wall-like ridges which separate the valleys while east-west movement depends on painful climbs to elevated cols in the crestline, which are snow-blocked in the winter months.

These conditions fostered the development of local loyalties and introspective parochial attitudes with resultant attachment to traditional practices and conservative outlook. Natural conditions also favoured defence and central and western Corsica may be regarded as a natural bastion against outside influences throughout history. The environment also set limits on economic possibilities, permanent agriculture being restricted to the valley floors and the littoral, dense forests dominating the slopes, while the pastures of the summits provided rough grazing in summer for sheep and goats. The crystalline mountains thus nurtured a pastoral economy with an associated patriarchal society, apt to administer its own summary form of justice and prone to political

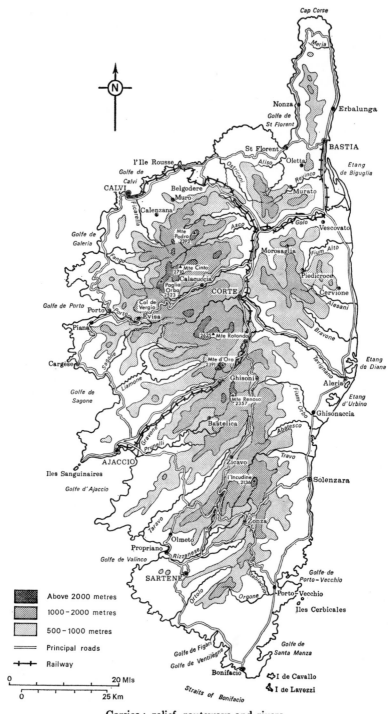

Corsica: relief, routeways and rivers

instability as a result of rivalry and intrigue between the constituent clans.

The Alpine earth movements which gave the crystalline rocks their present mountainous character also brought into existence a second mountain system. In the east, titanic forces thrust sediments against the more stable crystalline mountain mass, compressing them into fold structures and at the same time, through the generation of heat and pressure, causing a metamorphosis of the sediments into resistant schist rocks. The result was to weld on to the crystalline mountains a less extensive but more complex system of fold mountains which forms a major range in the northeastern third of the island. This chain begins at Cap Corse in the north as a simple arch of rocks forming a single ridge. Further south, the chain widens out into a complex of contorted rock structures forming the mountains of the Castagniccia. This zone is almost as rugged as the crystalline mountains but is lower in altitude and more open in relief, and is pierced by two major rivers, the Golo and the Tavignano, which offer relatively easy through-routes. Being lower than the crystalline ranges, these mountains were formerly wooded to their summits and, although slopes are everywhere steep, soils are more fertile than in the interior and could support more widespread crop growing.

The folded chains of the north-eastern range also offered refuge, not only from outside attack, but also from the malaria which used to infest the coastal lowlands. On the other hand, they have been more affected by outside influences than has the interior, a result both of the greater ease of penetration and, more especially, of their juxtaposition to the Tyrrhenian Sea and contact with the trade routes of the city states of the mainland. By contrast, the natural communication lines of the crystalline mountain ranges were orientated towards the void of the western Mediterranean basin. Equally significant, the better soils, the profusion of forests and the milder climate, enhanced the economic potential of the Castagniccia as compared with the limited possibilities of the interior. The chestnut forests nourished both animal and human populations and supported artisan industries. The

15

vine and olive were successfully introduced and cereals were grown on the terraced hillsides. The combination of livestock grazing, tree crops, cereals and craft industry supported a much greater population than was possible in the interior and the network of hilltop villages that was established in the Castagniccia produced the highest rural population densities in the island. Although differing little in general temperament from the Corsicans of the interior, the villagers of the Castagniccia have been more continuously involved, because of the existence of early trading connections and direct contact with external powers, in events extending beyond the island.

The contact between Corsica's two mountain systems, the predominantly granitic dissected masses of the west and interior and the folded schist chains of the north-east, is marked by a narrow depression that runs as a central furrow from north to south. It comprises a series of basins and portions of river valleys, separated by low cols. This central furrow has acted as a natural north-south routeway in which important settlements developed at the centres of the larger fertile lowland basins and also at the intersection with east-west routes. The prime example of these is Corte, situated at the island's major crossroads, while further north Ponte-Leccia occupies a similar strategic situation. Permitting relatively easy communication, the central furrow and its connecting valley routes also formed the natural line for troop movements and many of the island's most significant battles were inevitably fought in this zone.

The insistence that Corsica is not merely 'a mountain in the sea' but two different mountain systems may appear pedantic, but the contrast extends beyond geological differences. Since early times the Corsicans have distinguished between *L'En-deçà des Monts*, referring to the eastern third of the island, and *L'Au-delà des Monts*, applied to the crystalline mountains west of the central furrow. The distinction is between the eastern portion of the island, which successively was subjected to the colonising influence of Rome, Pisa and Genoa and where social evolution in favour of individual freedom advanced more surely,

Page 17 The mountain road through Corsican pines in the Forest of Aitone

Page 18 Typical maquis on a dry and rocky hillside

and the interior and west, where external control was more tenuous—at times nominal only—and the autocratic powers of feudal seigneurs were more persistent. The events of the twentieth century have done much to reduce these contrasts in the face of a common experience of economic decline and depopulation, but an understanding of the landscape, history and culture of Corsica depends on an appreciation of the physical and social divergence between the *banda di fuoro* of the interior and the *banda di dentro* of the east.

THE SEA

At first sight, the sea would appear to have had less effect in Corsican life than the mountain. Unlike many island races, the Corsicans have not become great seafarers, few ports animate the island's coast and the fishing industry is only a minor factor in the economy. In other respects the sea has played a determining role in the island's evolution, although the balance sheet of profit and loss is difficult to assess. By sea came the main civilising influences—Christianity, Pisan and Genoese culture, the impetus to urban life, the French language and administration—but there also came barbarian incursions and the mercenary troops of the great powers. Moreover the insularity of Corsica in large measure precipitated the island's economic decline.

The sea appears to have evoked a hesitant response from the Corsican. Fearing the exposure to external attack and shunning the malarial lowlands, the Corsicans built their villages on the hilltops and mountain slopes overlooking the sea and only established small *marines* or *cala* at the coast as fishing anchorages and temporary hamlets for seasonal livestock grazing. Permanent coastal towns did not make their appearance until the Genoese period, when a chain of fortified citadelles was built, the precursors of the present generation of port towns. It is only in the present century that the coast has come into its own, while the mountain civilisation is in strong regression. The coastal swamps have been cleared of malaria and are being actively reclaimed for modern irrigated agriculture. The towns of Bastia and Ajaccio depend on their ports now that the island has to make good its deficiencies in food supplies and almost every form of consumer goods by importing from the mainland. Whether by boat or by air, the tourists arrive at the coast and mostly choose to remain there amidst climatic conditions and coastal scenery of great attractiveness.

That the island has become increasingly orientated towards the coast reflects two circumstances; the decay of the traditional mountain economy and the emergence of Corsica from its brooding introspection to absorb attitudes, investment, technology and tourists from the mainland of Europe. Contrary to the usual progression of development, it is the coast which has become the new frontier while the interior betrays ever more signs of obsolescence. This transition is not being achieved without difficulties for the Corsican, for in the mountains are embedded the authentic culture and traditional attitudes.

The coastal zone is increasingly subjected to alien values, where the brash commercial influences of mainland France and cosmopolitan tourism confront an older society. Here huge apartment complexes now house families that were until recently shepherds and peasants. Increasingly the coast is becoming a façade composed of new elements in Corsican life—a sizeable urban proletariat, a growing bourgeoisie, and a generation of young Corsicans born not in remote villages but in modern clinics. This new generation finds its idols less in the heroic figures of Corsican history than in the current pop stars and sporting personalities. Educated in modern lycées and exposed by television to a broader horizon and wider spectrum of life than any previous generation, many leave to seek their fortunes on the mainland. In this they follow the example of previous generations of young Corsicans who became mercenaries in the armies of Europe and later, after French annexation, minor civil servants. Behind the coastal façade is the true Corsica, the Corsica of both heroic and tragic figures, of murderous battles and pitiless vendettas in the island's stormy history.

As yet the coastal façade of modern development is discontinuous. Only around the bays of Ajaccio and Calvi, in the agglomeration of Bastia, on the reclaimed portions of the eastern plain, and at isolated coastal tourist centres does the intrusion of new activities and settlement achieve significant proportions.

The coastline itself is far from uniform in character. A two-fold physical distinction may be made between the Mediterranean and Tyrrhenian coasts. On the western, Mediterranean coasts, the mountains abut directly on to the sea, giving spectacular cliff scenery with only isolated patches of coastal lowland. The dominant feature is the pattern of deeply embayed gulfs, formed when the foundering of the ancient land mass permitted the sea to invade the valleys. These former river courses are now represented as submarine canyons, 2,000 metres deep, which project the lines of the present-day valleys out to sea. This rugged type of coastline extends with little interruption from Cap Corse to Bonifacio. From the eastern base of Cap Corse the Tyrrhenian margin of the island has different characteristics. River erosion of the weaker schist rocks has permitted the accumulation of alluvial sediments which have built up a narrow coastal plain extending from Bastia to Solenzara. In contrast with the grandeur of the western coast, the Tyrrhenian coast is of monotonous regularity, overlooked by the forbidding mass of the Castagniccia several kilometres inland. The southern tip of the island introduces a miniature local variation in the form of the vertical limestone cliffs of Bonifacio. Here the dazzling white cliffs and deep grottoes recall the coast of Provence or of Malta.

ILE DE BEAUTÉ

The title 'a mountain in the sea', it has been suggested, is less exact than the more prosaic reality of two mountain systems set in two seas. The alternative slogan of the *Ile de Beauté* is less open to dispute, for if there is much that is sad about the island, the beauty of its landscape is beyond contradiction. The beauty of Corsica derives from the combination of spectacular moun-

21

tain and coastal scenery but it is the climate which enhances the landscape and adds further dimensions to the island's environment.

In very general terms Corsica has the characteristic Mediterranean climate of hot dry summers and mild wet winters, but this general pattern is subject to a number of influences which make for great variation within the island. The true Mediterranean climate is limited to the coastal zone, where the maritime influence exerts a tempering effect, moderating extremes of temperature. The chief factor modifying the climate is the effect of altitude but the detailed character of relief and aspect introduces further localised nuances in the form of microclimates. The typical Mediterranean climate close to sea level has the classic reverse patterns of temperature and rainfall. When the island is most cool rainfall is heaviest, and conversely the highest temperatures coincide with the period of lowest rainfall. The lowest temperatures occur in January and December, with mean values of approximately 9°C. Thereafter there is a gradual increase in temperature until March, which has an average of approximately 11°C. The temperature rises more rapidly in April, May and June and after a brief spring the long hot summer season is established. The highest temperatures are recorded in July and August, with means of 24°C and extremes of 30°C not uncommon. High temperatures persist into September but a rapid cooling occurs in October and November. Snowfall is rare and ephemeral at the coast, but frost is not entirely absent and occasionally damage to fruit crops can be severe. The rhythm of rainfall follows the reverse sequence, being heaviest in October and November with a second maximum in March. The total amount of winter rainfall at the coast averages 180mm. By contrast from June until September the drought may be almost absolute, with little rain falling and that confined to a small number of rain days. Summer rainfall occurs as stormy downpours separated by long dry spells. The intensity of the summer drought tends to increase from the north to the south.

Since the coastal lowlands are so limited in extent, very little of the island in fact experiences an unmodified Mediterranean climate. The general effect of increased altitude is to reduce the summer temperatures, to increase winter precipitation (with a high proportion falling as snow), and so to lower winter temperatures that frost is both common and widespread. The climatic contrast between the coast and the mountain interior is not, of course, abrupt. There is a gradual transition as the altitude increases but at places above 1,000m the climate must be considered as substantially different from that of the coast. Although the same seasonal rhythm is apparent, the total annual precipitation may reach 1,500mm and includes a snow cover lasting from 20 to 50 days. Above 2,000m annual precipitation totals over two metres and snow cover may persist for more than 140 days. These generalisations do not take account of variations brought about by aspect and local relief. Thus the deep valleys of the interior escape the effect of altitude and have rainfall totals closer to those of the coast.

The prevailing winds are those of the north-west, west and south-west, named the *Mistral* or *Libeccio*. Crossing large expanses of sea, these winds bring heavy rainfall to the western mountains but have spent most of their moisture before they reach the eastern coast. Rain is brought to the eastern coast by winds from the south (the *Sirocco*), from the east (the *Levante*), and from the north-east (the *Grecale*). These winds concentrate their winter rainfall in the east, for the mountain wall rises more abruptly here as compared with the more gradual increase in height from the western coasts. The northern coast is subject to the dry *Tramonte* wind, and when the mistral blows from the north it collects little moisture in its short sea crossing and gives little rain. For this reason, the northern coast has conditions drier than any other part of Corsica, other than the extreme south.

Although it experiences winds from several quarters, Corsica is by no means a windswept island. In the summer months, the daily land and sea breezes are of greater consequence. In the course of a summer morning the land heats up more rapidly than the sea, initiating a sea breeze. By late afternoon the pressure difference between land and sea is small and the air is calm. After sunset, the land loses heat more rapidly than the sea and a land breeze, the *u tarranu* blows; before the advent of motors, this breeze aided the fishing boats to put out to sea.

The climate is at once both an asset and a liability to Corsica. On the positive side the climate close to the sea—which affects the majority of the population today—must be considered extremely pleasant. If the summer heat imposes a rather lethargic rhythm to life in that season, autumn and spring can be idyllic while the winter is generally mild. Its mountainous character means that, away from the coast, Corsica is one of the most humid of Mediterranean islands. The ample precipitation and melting snow provide the island with abundant water supplies which can be stored to offset the summer drought, and the availability of stored water permits summer irrigation of crops during a season which otherwise becomes a virtual rest period for vegetative growth. In the upland interior the abundance of moisture, combined with lower temperatures, gives rise to a profuse vegetation which includes important expanses of forest. The range of climatic conditions enables Corsican agriculture to produce a bewildering variety of commodities, including citrus fruit and soft fruit at the coast, vines and olives on the lower slopes, and sweet chestnuts and timber products on the mountain flanks, while livestock can be grazed on the high pastures above the tree line. Finally, the certainty of fine weather throughout a prolonged summer gives the island ideal conditions for tourism, and the heavy snowfall a potential—as yet not fully developed—for winter sports holidays.

Against these obvious advantages must be ranged certain limitations. Because of the seasonal nature of rainfall and the need for irrigation during the summer months, elaborate and costly water storage and distribution systems have to be installed. In the conditions of deficient summer rainfall, the lower natural pasture becomes scorched, forcing the migration of livestock to the mountain grazings where the pasture is extensive but has a low carrying capacity. The heat of summer makes for a general somnolence and a characteristic 'Mediterranean' pace of life. In winter, on the other hand, the heavy snowstorms commonly close the mountain passes, isolating the east from the west, except via the single rail link which tunnels beneath the Col de Vizzavona. Finally, the climate of Corsica is prone to natural disasters of various kinds, from avalanches and spectacular forest fires to violent storms and damaging frosts. Nevertheless, on balance the climate must be considered as probably the island's most valuable resource, and it provides a more favourable environment for settlement and economic development than that of almost any other Mediterranean island.

THE SCENTED ISLE

The title of 'the scented isle' alludes to the strong perfume exuded by the aromatic vegetation of the island, which on occasion is even perceptible at some distance from the shore. Moreover the beauty of the landscape is enhanced by the visual effect of the vegetation, be it the radiant colours of the maquis at spring flowering, the majestic loneliness of the mountain pine forests or the pastel shadings of the chestnut woods of the Castagniccia. Apart from the appeal to the senses, the vegetation has much intrinsic interest. The profusion and rich variety of the species, ranging from drought-resistant cacti, reminiscent of North Africa, to miniature alpine plants, makes the island a botanist's treasure house. It is estimated that there are at least 78 species of plants which are found only in Corsica, 32 species which are variants of plants found elsewhere, and over 100 species which are not found in mainland France.

The vegetation has an economic potential sadly underused at the present time. In the coastal zone a wide range of citrus fruits flourish, oranges, clementines, lemons and cedrats, accompanied by such soft fruits as peaches and apricots. On the lower hill slopes vines are grown, almonds flourish and vast olive groves are untended and for the most part no longer harvested. On the mountains extensive forests of pine, beech and fir have suffered

25

from neglect, haphazard exploitation and the ravages of fires. The vegetation has played an important part in the island's history. One may cite the role of the chestnut in the support of the peasant economy of the Castagniccia, and the deliberate destruction of the chestnut groves by the Genoese in an effort to deprive this bastion of Corsican opposition of its food supplies. The present degraded state of the vegetation speaks volumes on the island's history of unrest, neglect and deliberate abandonment.

It is impossible to generalise the pattern of the plant life satisfactorily, for such conditions as aspect in relation to insolation and wind, variations in slope, rock type, soil mantle, and even the historical events of a particular village or valley are all reflected in local variations in vegetation which compose an inextricable mosaic. It is possible to classify the natural vegetation in altitudinal zones in relation to climate and relief. Within each altitudinal zone, specific associations of plants and trees represent the final natural adjustment to the prevalent climatic conditions.

Below 600m, where the true Mediterranean climate prevails, the natural forest cover consists of cork oak (*Quercus suber*) and evergreen oak (*Q. ilex*), mixed with maritime pine (*Pinus pinaster*) and umbrella pine (*P. pinea*). In fact little remains of this natural forest. The chief surviving example is the forest of Porto-Vecchio, but elsewhere the forest has been removed by clearance for agriculture and settlement, and degraded scrub has taken its place. On the other hand, many exotic species have been introduced to the coastal lowlands, especially the palm tree (*Chamaerops humilis*), planted for ornamental purposes, and the eucalyptus, planted on the low-lying plains where its capacity for absorbing moisture improves the drainage. At the coast too are to be found many of the island's most spectacular and bizarre plants, such as the agave, barbary fig, aloes and other succulents, which are intermingled with the scrub. Between 600m and 1,000m conditions are more humid as the lower temperatures reduce losses by evaporation. The natural forest cover is of maritime pine and pubescent oak (*Quercus pubescens*). The latter is now rare, having been largely usurped through the planting of sweet chestnut (*Castanea*). This tree is developed in pure stands in the Castagniccia where formerly it was carefully husbanded. In the areas where chestnut cultivation has been abandoned there is now a dense undergrowth of bracken. From 1,000m to approximately 1,800m, the mountain climate favours the growth of the Corsican pine (*Pinus laricio*), associated with beech (*Fagus sylvatica*) and firs (*Abies*). The Corsican pine provides the island with its most magnificent forests, especially those of Aitone and Vizzavona. Above 1,800m lies a pseudo-alpine zone extending to the mountain summits. Here dwarf alders (*Alnus suaveolens*) and junipers (*Juniperus communis*) give way to short grass in which grow many varieties of low-growing alpine flowers.

Although this idealised zonation represents the natural succession of vegetation types this sequence has been so interfered with by man's activities as to frustrate nature's tendency to maintain an orderly balance. The process of destruction has continued over the centuries as a result of the clearing of land for agriculture, cutting for timber and charcoal, indiscriminate burning, and the depredations of grazing livestock, especially goats. The removal of the natural forest cover has led to a secondary growth of a degraded vegetation type, the famous *maquis*, a term which is applied to an association of plants forming a dense scrub vegetation of varying heights, above which isolated clumps of taller trees often stand. The most common shrubs are arbutus (*Arbutus unedo*), lentisk (*Pistacia lentiscus*) and *Erica arborea*. Above the shrubs stand occasional patches of cork oak, evergreen oak and pine, and below them gorse (*Ulex europaens*), bracken (*pteridium*), broom (*Cystisus*) and thyme (*Thymus serpyllum*) form a confused herbaceous tangle. Where it is well developed the maquis forms an almost inpenetrable barrier, especially as the higher bushes often support spiny climbing plants. The vegetation is characterised by its adaptation to desiccation during the summer drought, the small narrow waxy leaves and the covering of hairs and spines all having evolved to reduce transpiration. The maquis is also characterised during spring and

27

early summer by the dazzling colours of its flowers and by the heady perfume which impregnates the air. It is estimated that the various forms of maquis cover almost three-quarters of the island and it certainly gives the island its overall aspect of a luxuriant vegetation and evergreen appearance.

The maquis is not always dense and impenetrable. It is on the more fertile soils, along watercourses, and on the abandoned fields of the lowlands that dense maquis is most prevalent. On the higher slopes, where it is frequently burned by shepherds to stimulate young shoots for grazing, a less profuse *petit maquis*, composed mainly of herbaceous undergrowth, is present. Nor is the maquis entirely lacking in economic value. It is used as firewood, its flowers support the production of honey, and the burnt vegetation adds some nutrient to the soil, thus stimulating grass growth for rough grazing. The indiscriminate burning is on the whole an unfortunate practice, for it robs the environment of one of the principal benefits of the maquis, namely its role in providing dense plant cover which protects the soil from erosion. In summary, if the maquis may be taken as a symbol of the Corsican landscape, by virtue of its ubiquity, it is also symbolic of a misuse of land and forest resources. The maquis is an invader, which has replaced the destroyed forests and covered formerly productive fields.

2   CORSICAN LANDSCAPES

THE intense dissection of Corsica has produced a compart-
mentalisation of life within a mosaic of tiny regions, each
clearly defined physically, closely integrated socially and
having a particular history. The depopulation of the interior and
the decay of the rural economy are slowly eroding these subtle
regional variations in the landscape with their associated traditions, folk-lore and particularities of speech. Nevertheless, it is
still possible to distinguish a number of larger regions which still
retain their distinctive landscape and economy. This chapter seeks
to characterise the main contrasts in the landscape which unfold
before the traveller.

CAP CORSE

Cap Corse is the most clearly defined region of Corsica, a virtual
island within an island. Projecting northwards for a distance of
forty kilometres, the peninsula has an average width of approximately twelve kilometres. It has the most simple and symmetrical
relief of all the mountainous portion of the island. The rocks
are arched into a single fold which dips steeply to the west and
rather less steeply to the east from a central ridge. The crestline
consists of a tract of bare rock, mainly just below 1,000 metres
high, though several eminences rise above this altitude. The
highest summit, Monte Stello at 1,305m, commands one of the
finest views in the island, extending to the Tuscan archipelago
and the mainland of Italy to the east, the coastal plain and Castagniccia to the south, the Gulf of St Florent and the Balagne to
the west, and the mountain massifs of Cinto and Rotondo to the
south-west.

The mountain chain has been dissected by streams flowing

29

east and west from the crest, each of which has carved out a deep amphitheatre, open to the sea. These valleys are the chief inhabited areas and settlement takes the form of scattered hamlets loosely distributed about the main hillside villages, to which they are often connected only by tracks. In turn, each valley has its *marine*, a coastal hamlet located on the miniature bay at the outlet of the stream, and commonly overlooked by one of the Genoese watchtowers which punctuate the coast of the Cap.

The traces of former cultivated terraced fields, now overgrown by maquis, which extend far up the mountainsides are evidence of a past prosperity. Cap Corse has been described as a ruin—an allusion to its abandoned fields and houses, the large-scale depopulation and the decline of a once-varied economy. Centuries ago the Cap was a major area of viticulture and, unlike most Corsicans, the citizens of the Cap had come to terms with the sea. Venturing from their minute ports, they mastered the art of navigation, engaged in fishing, and above all became involved in trade. Located favourably in relation to the Italian mainland, the Cap traded not only its own produce but also became a kind of entrepôt for trade in the products of the Balagne and the interior.

Cap Corse became the most outward-looking part of the island and adjusted more readily to occupation by the Genoese. Fidelity to the Genoese, reinforced by privileges accorded by Genoa, enabled the seigneurs to prolong their sway, even after the declaration of the *Terre des Communes* elsewhere in eastern Corsica. The annexation of the island by France in the eighteenth century and the consequent rupture of the traditional trading connection with Genoa was but the first stage in the decline of the economy. The ravages of phylloxera in the vineyards towards the end of last century proved equally disastrous and heralded the outward movement of population which has proceeded unchecked to the present day. Agriculture has receded to patches of accessible land around the hamlets, livestock are no longer of great significance, and the maquis has spread down the mountain slopes to sea level. The main exception is the persistence of viticulture in the north of the Cap around Rogliano, which produces the *Cap Corse* wines, among the most appreciated on the island. Fishing persists in a desultory manner, but an important mineral resource, the asbestos of Canari, is no longer mined.

Cap Corse is perhaps in most respects a ruin, in that the vestiges of a more vital past are everywhere in evidence, but it is not without some signs of evolution. The south-eastern portion of the Cap is increasingly falling within the orbit of Bastia and the hamlets in the communes of St Martin di Lota and Brando now accommodate a population of commuters who maintain a little land as smallholdings. The *marines* of these communes are being increasingly invaded by the development of villas built by the wealthier and retired classes of Bastia.

Another development results from the region's natural vocation as a tourist circuit. A serpentine road hugging the coast for approximately one hundred kilometres offers an ideal excursion, with continuous magnificent coastal and mountain vistas. The eastern coast is relatively straight and the road follows it virtually at sea level passing through a succession of delightful *marines*, of which Erbalunga, with its miniature harbour guarded by a ruined Genoese watchtower, is perhaps the most attractive. By contrast, the scenery of the west coast is more grandiose. The mountains plunge abruptly into the sea, the coastline is more indented and the road is carved into the mountainside as a spectacular corniche. The villages hang dramatically above the sea, perched like birds' nests on crags, none more so than the village of Nonza. The circuit is completed by crossing to Bastia via the Col de Teghime, with magnificent seaward views both to east and to west. The fact that the tour of the Cap can be completed leisurely in a day has preserved Cap Corse from the kinds of tourist development that would destroy its beauty. The occasional restaurant is the only evidence of a tourism which is essentially *en passant*.

Populated by no more than 5,000 inhabitants, Cap Corse is now a pale reflection of its past importance. The broad deep valleys of the east, sheltered from the predominant winds, contain large expanses of abandoned land, but there seems no likeli-

31

Corsica: physical features and regions

hood that it will ever be put to use again. The population has fallen below the limit capable of returning land to production and the Cap seems destined to remain a ruin, appreciated as a tourist spectacle, but too far decayed to permit an easy reconstruction.

NEBBIO

The huge arch of Cap Corse has a reverse image immediately to the west in the form of a downfolded basin. This basin has been partially invaded by the sea, in the Gulf of St Florent, but is continued inland as the Nebbio. The heart of the Nebbio is the broad lowland drained by the Aliso and its tributaries, but to the west and south-west the rocks arch up once more to form the Desert des Agriates and the mountain chain of Tenda. The essential characteristic of the Nebbio is therefore its enclosed nature, an enclave of productive lowland within a screen of almost empty and unproductive upland—a garden in a wilderness. The unity afforded by the natural boundaries of mountain and sea has been recognised throughout history. The Nebbio since antiquity has been considered as a *piève*, a social and administrative unit, a fact recognised in ecclesiastical terms by its designation as a bishopric, and in strategic terms by its organisation as a military unit under the Genoese, commanded from their citadelle in St Florent.

The Aliso basin is by no means a level plain, but rather an area of fragmented relief with frequent changes in slope, aspect and soil conditions. These variations account for the relatively productive nature of agriculture. Conditions are propitious for a wide range of activities. The valley floors support pasture and tree crops, the lower slopes are devoted to vines and the maquis and rough pasture of the higher slopes supply grazing for sheep and goats. The main commercial enterprise is viticulture, producing a wine of good quality and high alcohol content, the *Patrimonio*. The variety of land use produces a patchwork landscape and, in general, a garden appearance—even if at times the garden has become overgrown by the invading maquis.

33

Whereas Cap Corse is a cul-de-sac, the Nebbio does have a strong internal focus in the shape of the miniature capital St Florent. Situated at the mouth of the Aliso, the town commands a magnificent panorama of the Gulf of St Florent. Essentially a Genoese creation, St Florent was one of the citadelles which punctuated the Corsican coastline. The fifteenth-century citadelle replaced an existing settlement of Nebbio, a Roman foundation approximately one kilometre to the east. Of this old settlement, abandoned after the creation of the citadelle, only the cathedral remains, dating from the thirteenth century. Built in the Romanesque style it has three naves and bears a close architectural resemblance to the more famous Canonica, on the site of the Roman town of Mariana, south of Bastia.

The modern town of St Florent huddles beneath the circular Genoese citadelle and extends along the sea front towards the Aliso. The combination of its magnificent setting on the Gulf of St Florent, the attractiveness of the town's waterfront and fishing harbour, the good beaches and the creation of a yachting marina accounts for the recent increase in the number of tourists visiting the town. The permanent population is less than one thousand, but the town's function as the centre for a productive agricultural hinterland and its strategic position in relation to tourist routes suggest that a potential for growth is present.

Few more impressive contrasts exist in Corsica than that between the verdant landscape of the Nebbio basin, and the stark desolation of the adjacent upland. This is particularly the case to the west, where the bulging foreland of the Désert des Agriates introduces a landscape which is almost lunar in its desolation. The name *désert* refers both to the extreme shortage of water and to the virtual emptiness of the region. Jagged hills, rising to an average of 300m, are barren but for a stunted maquis scrub, and human habitation is practically non-existent. The low hills are an insufficient barrier to intercept the rain-bearing winds and to cause them to drop their moisture, and as a consequence this is one of the driest portions of the island. Further south, the more elevated range of the Tenda has a more abundant rainfall and

Page 35 A hillside village among terraced fields in the Balagne, north-west Corsica

Page 36 Aerial view of mountain and plain in eastern Corsica, where the Castagniccia meets the Marana lowland a number of agricultural villages line the Ostriconi valley to the west and also the eastern flank of the Tenda range. The total population of the Nebbio and its surrounding upland is little more than 3,000, of which an increasing proportion is accounted for by St Florent.

THE BALAGNE

The rolling hills and plains of the Balagne form a smiling oasis of civilisation surrounded by altogether more hostile and empty territory. The region is unique in the island, an area of alternating hills and broad valleys hemmed in by the ramparts of the towering Monte Grosso and Cinto ranges. The Balagne extends from south of Calvi to the mouth of the Ostriconi river and stretches inland some ten kilometres to Belgodere and Calenzana. It is the most diversified of the smaller regions of Corsica and its charm springs from the frequent variation in landscape and the aura of civilisation that results from the patchwork of terraced fields and plantations, the numerous hilltop villages and the towns of the coast.

The Balagne has a long history of civilisation, as testified by prehistoric and Roman remains, the Genoese fortresses of Calvi and Algajola, and the Corsican 'new town' of l'Ile-Rousse built by the patriot Paoli in the eighteenth century. The attraction of the region was primarily the fertility of the valleys, where cereals, vine and olives prospered, while the hill lands supported forests and grazing. Like the Castagniccia, the Balagne was able to develop a self-sufficient economy and to sustain a high rural population density. Unlike the Castagniccia, the Balagne has open terrain, drained to the sea by broad valleys, which made incursion easy. This was one of the principal areas of Moorish invasion and, at a later date, a stronghold of the Genoese occupation. The result of this background of prosperity, ease of movement and assimilation of numerous foreign elements has been to give the inhabitants, at least in the eyes of fellow Corsicans, a calmer, more reflective and more peaceable temperament.

In modern times, the Balagne has shared the island's economic

c

decline, and the hilltop villages, for all their picturesque setting, now house only a proportion of their former populations. With the collapse of traditional farming, the greater part of the agricultural land has been abandoned. Farming has survived best in the larger valleys, where irrigation has permitted reclamation and plantation-style production. South of Calvi, the Ficarella plain is being irrigated for both crops and pasture. Viticulture and cattle rearing are still important and the little town of Calenzana, built where the Balagne meets the mountains, is the capital for this productive farming area. In the east, the Ostriconi valley is the site of a revival of olive cultivation in a co-operative scheme. Between the Ficarella and the Ostriconi valleys, the heart of the Balagne is virtually an overgrown garden. The terraced fields have been invaded by maquis and former cropland is now rented out as pasture to shepherds who market their ewe's milk via the Roquefort dairy at l'Ile-Rousse. The degree of agricultural degeneration is less than that of Cap Corse, but depopulation is severe. The main interest for the visitor is the classic circuit of central Balagne, from l'Ile-Rousse or Calvi via Belgodere and Muro. The route follows a corniche that links a succession of hilltop villages, each commanding magnificent vistas of the coast and backed by the mountain panorama of the forested Monte Grosso range.

As compared with interior Balagne, the coast has experienced a rapid economic development. Even before the last war, Calvi was a favoured tourist centre while l'Ile-Rousse boasted the island's only luxury hotel. Between 1960 and 1970 tourism burgeoned not only in these two places, but also at intervals along the coast between them. New hotels, holiday villages and private villas have been built east of Calvi, at Algajola and at l'Ile-Rousse. The coast has become, at least in the summer months, a holiday playground, with an accent on informality, marine sports and animated night life. There seems little doubt that this playground function will be expanded, for no other section of the island can boast the same combination of amenities: excellent beaches, historic citadelles and churches, a picturesque hinterland and immediate access to some of the highest mountain ranges.

LA CASTAGNICCIA

La Castagniccia, which takes its name from the dense chestnut forests that garb its slopes, is perhaps the most fascinating region of Corsica. The chestnut not only dominates the landscape, it also symbolises a past way of life. For centuries, the chestnut provided flour for both human consumption and export and a foodstuff for pigs. The combination of the chestnut with vines and olives on the lower slopes, vegetable gardens around the villages, the grazing of pigs in the chestnut groves and that of sheep and goats on the maquis, made for a high degree of self-sufficiency in the economy and permitted dense village settlement to be established.

The Castagniccia lies between the Golo and Tavignano rivers, and is structurally an extension of the schist rocks of Cap Corse. The structure is much more complex however, and instead of a single arch, there is a succession of folded and fractured rocks, which have been deeply eroded by powerful streams. The mountains are not high, the highest peak San Petrone being 1,766m, but everywhere slopes are steep and the relief is generally rugged. The rivers radiate outwards from the heart of the Castagniccia, so that, with the exception of the Golo and Tavignano corridors, through-routes are possible only by dint of crossing high cols approached through narrow defiles. As a consequence, the Castagniccia is a natural fortress, and has traditionally been a bastion of Corsican resistance and patriotism. The great patriot Pascal Paoli was born in Morosaglia, in the heart of the Castagniccia. The network of valleys, each providing a variety of land resources, promoted village development on a greater scale than elsewhere in the island. Most of the settlements lie between 600 and 800m, at the margin of the chestnut forest and safe from the ravages of malaria and from surprise attack. On the eastern flank, a distinct chain of villages at this altitude overlooks the Tyrrhenian sea, linked by a sinuous corniche of roads and tracks.

In spite of the proliferation of settlement, no towns grace the Castagniccia. Piedicroce is the principal centre but has fewer than 300 permanent inhabitants. In many ways it typifies the thriving past and the present decadence of the region. At the beginning of the century, Piedicroce was an active centre of artisan industries; woodworking based on oak, beech, and briar, iron working for utensils and agricultural equipment, leather working and pottery making. The stability of an economy based largely on the chestnut forests gave time and opportunity for crafts to develop and made the Castagniccia virtually the only part of the island with a tradition of artisan skills. Now little remains of these craft industries. The chestnut groves have decayed through the ravages of ink disease (a lethal fungus infection), careless management and over-exploitation, and, above all, the population of the Castagniccia has been decimated by emigration.

More than any other region, the Castagniccia portrays the magnitude of the island's economic and demographic decline. The hilltop villages, perched on their natural lookouts, are fast decaying and many of the outlying hamlets have been totally abandoned and their ruins engulfed by the advancing maquis. A meagre population, mostly elderly, survives to work the gardens around the villages and graze a few livestock, but everywhere, the inexorable march of the maquis over once cultivated fields continues. Year by year, the chestnut groves deteriorate and a once noble economy, fulfilling the everyday needs of a dense population, is slowly dying. Yet, if the inhabitants of the Castagniccia have not hesitated to emigrate to better opportunities on the continent, they have also remained faithful to their origin. They return to their native villages each year for holidays, to vote in elections and for ultimate retirement. There is thus a great discrepancy in numbers between the dwindling permanent population and the much larger summer population. This brings some transformation from the eerie emptiness of the villages throughout most of the year to something approaching animation during the summer holiday period.

While the decline of interior and western Corsica is perhaps easy to accept, for population density was never high and physical conditions are so obviously restrictive, the decay of the Castagniccia is more poignant. Here not only a population but also a culture is in the process of obliteration. The east-flowing rivers, notably the Fium' Alto, Fium' Orbo and Alesani, are the scene of new storage dams, but this is to benefit the eastern coastal plains where a new landscape and culture are emerging. The contrast between an age-old way of life, cradled in the chestnut-covered mountains, and the twentieth-century landscape now being established on the plains at the foot of the Castagniccia is without doubt the most striking antithesis in Corsica's rural landscapes.

THE EASTERN PLAINS

Between Bastia and Solenzara, a distance of a hundred kilometres, stretches Corsica's only substantial area of lowland. Even this is not continuous but is broken up by belts of hills. In particular a distinction may be made between the areas to the north and south of the Alesani river, at which point the Castagniccia extends to within a few kilometres of the sea, separating the narrow plain south of Bastia from the much more extensive triangular lowland of the Plain of Aleria.

Immediately south of the citadelle at Bastia, the rocky coast of Cap Corse gives way to a regular coastline, bordered by dunes. Behind the dunes lies the narrow plain of Marana, which extends from Bastia to the mouth of the Golo, site of the Roman settlement of Mariana and the precursor of the modern port and town of Bastia. The plain has several singular features, notably the precipitous mountain wall on its inland edge and the vast lagoon (*étang*) of Biguglia separated from the sea by a narrow sand spit. The mountain wall has a line of hillside villages, occupying 'balcony' sites that were safe from the dual threats of malaria and attack on this, the most exposed flank of the island. These villages have some distinction whether for the magnificence of their sites, such as Brando and Furiani, or for their historical association;

Biguglia was the capital of the popular uprising, the *Terre des Communes*, in the fifteenth century and had earlier been a Pisan stronghold. All have now fallen under the influence of Bastia and, far from decaying, these settlements have witnessed some new building.

The plain is currently the site of several economic changes and rapid progress. It was formerly prone to flooding, but this risk has been removed by drainage canals, lined by eucalyptus trees and bamboo. Market gardening is important and new fruit farms are being established with the aid of irrigation water taken from the Golo river. Precluded from expansion north and west by the mountains, the agglomeration of Bastia has spilled out on to the plain in the form of large housing estates and an almost continuous ribbon development along the coast road. Further developments are small-scale industries and depots on the road between Bastia and the expanding airport fifteen kilometres to the south, the establishment of a new tourist complex on the sandspit of the lagoon, and the creation of a huge fruit canning factory on the banks of the Golo. The combination of commuters, traffic destined for the port and airport, and tourists has made the coast road between the Golo and Bastia the most congested highway in the island. The fact that the road is level and straight permits speeds unattainable elsewhere in the island, with consequent suicidal tendencies among drivers.

Another feature of the plain is the site of the Roman town and port of Mariana, close to the mouth of the Golo. Vestiges of the town remain, close by the cathedral of La Canonica. This edifice, built in the twelfth century, is the finest example of Pisan architecture in the island, and now stands in isolation at the perimeter of Bastia airport.

South of the Golo river, the mountain wall is interrupted by a number of valleys and a narrow foothill zone fronts the Castagniccia. The name Casinca is applied to the plain and foothills between the Golo and the Alesani rivers. The commune boundaries traverse the foothills and plain giving to each community a variety of land resources. In the foothills olive and citrus trees are found, giving way on the coastal plain to pasture, vineyards, soft fruits and market garden crops. This small sub-region is one of the most favoured portions of the island, having good alluvial soils and access to the precious commodity of water in summer from storage dams. Traditionally the farmers used to have a house in the hillside village and a second building on the plain. The modern tendency is for the villages to decline in importance, and for the farms on the plain to assume a permanent character. The explanation lies in the expansion of irrigation facilities and the clearing of new land on the plain, which permit an intensification of agriculture. The Casinca has thus resisted depopulation to a greater extent than elsewhere in rural Corsica and, on the contrary, attracts a seasonal influx of workers from abroad during the harvest period. The region lacks towns but Moriani Plage has become the focus of coastal tourism.

South of the Alesani river, the coastal plain widens into a triangular lowland, the *Piaddia d'Aleria* or Plain of Aleria. Until after the second World War the plain was largely a 'negative' area. The coastal lagoons and the swampy outlets of the rivers were breeding grounds of malaria. Most of the land was communally owned by the villagers of the surrounding hills and served merely as winter grazing. The intensity of the drought together with the risk of malaria precluded any productive use in the summer months, and maquis scrub covered virtually the whole plain.

The plain had witnessed a more distinguished past, for here the Romans built their most substantial town and port, Aleria, and the surrounding plains provided grain for export. The collapse of Roman control and the appearance of endemic malaria extinguished this civilisation and indeed most of the permanent settlement. Raised on a pronounced eminence above the plain, Aleria survived as a settlement, perpetuating the earlier Greek and Roman towns, but with only 500 inhabitants at present it has scarcely retained its historic importance. The role of capital of the Plain of Aleria has been taken over by Ghisonaccia, on the left bank of the Fium' Orbo. A small town of almost 2,000 inhabitants, Ghisonaccia owes its recent development to the impressive government-sponsored reclamation programme which is transforming the plain. The storage of water in new reservoirs has permitted the irrigation of entirely new plantations carved out of the maquis, growing vines, citrus and soft fruit. Developed initially by repatriates from North Africa, this represents an anomaly in the Corsican landscape—an advancing frontier of agriculture and settlement, as opposed to the more widespread pattern of retreat and decay.

THE NIOLO

Niolo, meaning 'land of the clouds', is the name of the most elevated portion of Corsica, covering the upper basins of the Golo, Tavignano, and their tributaries. It is at once the most inaccessible, inhospitable and yet most beautiful mountain region of Corsica—inhospitable because here are found the island's highest peaks and wildest gorges, inaccessible because the valley heads are enclosed amphitheatres above which tower like sentinels jagged summits at between 2,000m and 2,500m. Only one road crosses the Niolo, from the valley of the Golo to that of the Porto, via the Col de Vergio, which at over 1,400 metres is the island's highest road. The 'land of the clouds' refers to the height of the mountains, which are frequently clothed in cloud, as are the villages, which, at between 800m and 1,000m, are the highest in Corsica. In view of the inaccessibility and isolation, and the limitations on economic activity imposed by the mountains, it is not surprising that in the Niolo traditional ways of life have persisted.

The Niolo consists essentially of a number of parallel valleys draining to the Golo and the Tavignano and separated by high mountain barriers that are traversed only by tracks. Access is also impeded by the deep incision of the rivers which run in narrow gorges that guard the entry to the upper portions of the valleys. Thus the gorges of the Asco restrict access to the village of Asco, the spectacular Scala di Santa Regina guards the approach to the upper Golo valley, the village of Calacuccia and the Col de Vergio. Similar gorges occur in the upper Tavignano valley and its tributary the Restonica. The upper reaches of the valleys are swathed in immense forests, above which lie the high summer pastures devoid of all settlement other than shepherds' huts and remote stone shelters.

The most imposing valleys scenically are those of the Asco and the Golo. The Asco valley lies between the Monte Padro and Monte Cinto ranges and rises in the Forest of Carozicca. Asco is a settlement of some 400 inhabitants with a setting that is virtually alpine. In addition to its pastoral economy, Asco is the principal centre for mountaineering, being the best point of departure for the ascent of Monte Padro (2,393m), Monte Cinto (2,710m) and Capo Bianco (2,554m). It is also the scene of Corsica's first winter sports development. The upper Golo valley separates the Cinto range from the Forest of Valdo-Niello, and in Calacuccia, it posssesses the miniature capital of the Niolo— with a thousand inhabitants this is little more than a shepherd village. It has a pleasant setting amidst chestnut groves and is the site of an important new water storage barrage. Monte Cinto and Paglia Orba (2,523m) are accessible from Calacuccia but the town's major function as the centre of the Niolo results from its situation on the only through road, via the Col de Vergio, to the west coast of the island.

South of the Golo valley the upper Tavignano and Restonica rivers drain the large area, devoid of village settlement, that comprises the Monte Rotondo range. Its jagged outlines etched out by past glaciation, Monte Rotondo (2,625m) is perhaps a more impressive peak than Monte Cinto. Tracks lead through magnificent forests to lakes on its upper flanks, above which rises the vertiginous summit of the mountain.

The economy of the Niolo rests firmly on pastoralism and on seasonal rhythms of livestock movements which have changed little over the centuries. Throughout the harsh winter months when snow covers the mountains and blocks the passes, the livestock are moved to coastal lowlands. The most important migra-

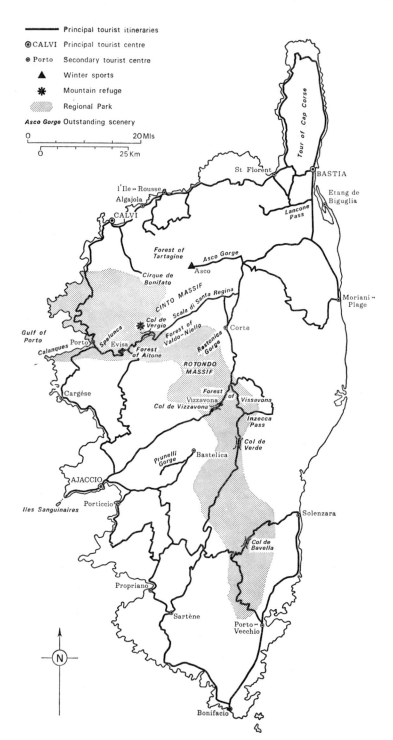

Principal tourist itineraries

⊚CALVI Principal tourist centre

⊚ Porto Secondary tourist centre

▲ Winter sports

✳ Mountain refuge

Regional Park

Asco Gorge Outstanding scenery

0   20 Mls

0   25 Km

Tour of Cap Corse

St Florent

BASTIA

Etang de Biguglia

l'Ile ~ Rousse

Algajola

CALVI

Lancone Pass

Forest of Tartagine

Asco Gorge

Asco

Cirque de Bonifato

CINTO MASSIF

Scala di Santa Regina

Moriani ~ Plage

Col de Vergio

Forest of Valdo~Niello

Corte

Gulf of Porto

Porto

Spelunca

Evisa

Forest of Aitone

Rastonica Gorge

Calanques

ROTONDO MASSIF

Cargèse

Forest of Vizzavona

Vissavona

Col de Vizzavona

Inzecca Pass

Col de Verde

Prunelli Gorge

Bastelica

AJACCIO

Porticcio

Iles Sanguinaires

Solenzara

Col de Bavella

Propriano

Sartène

Porto ~ Vecchio

N

Bonifacio

Corsica : tourist features

tions are westwards to the lowlands of Galeria in the valley of the Fango and northwards to the Balagne, but lesser migrations occur eastwards via the Tavignano valley as far as the Plain of Aleria. In summer the pattern is reversed, the shepherds returning to the mountains to graze their livestock on the alpine pastures above the tree line. The principal enterprise is the raising of sheep for ewe's milk to be sold for cheese making but several thousand cattle, pigs and goats also graze on the valley floors and the mountain pastures. The extensive nature of the economy requires a small labour force in relation to the large area of land involved and only a dozen or so villages are to be found in the Niolo. The mountain pastures are devoid of permanent settlement but are dotted with sheep folds (*bergeries*), shepherds' huts built of stone and occupied only during the summer, and, on the highest pastures, pyramidal stone shelters.

Having an economy based on methods which have changed little and with a guaranteed outlet for animal produce, the Niolo shows less sign of decay than those parts of the island, such as Cap Corse and the Castagniccia, where a more intensive agriculture was formerly present. As yet tourism has not intruded unduly into the landscape. Problems of access limit tourism mainly to mountain climbing and naturalist study, which merely emphasise the general alpine character of the economy. Only Asco can be considered as an embryonic resort, and for the present at least, the wild life, the forests, the tranquillity and the breathtaking scenery remain undisturbed.

THE CINARCA

Between the valleys of the west-flowing Porto and Prunelli rivers, high mountain ridges alternate with deep valleys, the former terminating as prominent coastal headlands and the latter as impressive gulfs. The heart of this diverse region is the Cinarca, domain of the fabled Cinarchese family. The Cinarca is more specifically the area drained by the Liamone, Cruzzini and Liscia rivers. Here the Cinarchese family established its feudal reign and for over 250 years, the Counts of Cinarca dominated the island. Aristocrats by common assent rather than by ancestral title, the family, frequently divided within itself rather than against the Genoese, supplied the island with a succession of heroes and tragic figures in roughly equal proportion. The Cinarca is generally lower than the Niolo and possesses less striking scenery. The valleys are wider and consequently the mountain pastures are more restricted. Nor does the Cinarca have large coastal plains accessible for winter grazing. The livestock population is much smaller than that of the Niolo and settlement density is low. The principal centre, Vico, has little more than a thousand inhabitants. The major road in the west follows the coast and the Cinarca is served only by extremely poor minor roads and tracks.

From a scenic viewpoint greater interest attaches to the neighbouring valleys to north and south, and to the coast. To the north of the Cinarca, the basin of the Porto possesses some of the finest scenery of the island. Rising in the magnificent Forêt d'Aitone, the Porto flows westwards into the most impressive of Corsica's gulfs. A right-bank tributary flows from the forest of Aitone through the Spelunca, surely the most savage of Corsica's gorges, to join the Porto near Evisa. Evisa is a pleasant settlement of 600 inhabitants, set in chestnut groves and an ideally placed centre from which to explore the Spelunca and the Forêt d'Aitone; via the Col de Vergio, it gives access to the high ranges of the Niolo. Near the mouth of the Porto, the small town of the same name commands the gulf. Its *marine*, guarded by a Genoese tower, has a small port and good beaches. Immediately to the south-west the Calanques de Piana present some of the most remarkable coastal scenery in Europe. Jagged pinnacles of vivid red granite surmount the cliffs which drop vertically over 250m to the sea.

To the south, the mountains of the Cinarca overlook the valley of the Gravone, an important corridor of movement from Ajaccio to Corte via the Col de Vizzavona. This route, followed by main road and rail, is an essential lifeline within the island, for even when the road is snow-blocked for long periods in winter, the railway line, by virtue of its tunnel cut beneath the col, remains open. The Col de Vizzavona lies between Monte d'Oro to the north (2,391m) and Monte Renoso to the south (2,357m). Because of its majestic isolation and perpendicular ramparts of bare granite, Monte d'Oro viewed from the south is perhaps the island's most imposing mountain. Vizzavona is the principal summer mountain resort in Corsica. Set at a height of 906m in a clearing in the magnificent forest of Vizzavona, the settlement offers an escape from the crushing heat of the sea-level towns, especially to the citizens of Ajaccio. South of the Gravone, the parallel valley of the Prunelli is not a major through-route but Bastelica, at the foot of Monte Renoso, is also a favoured summer resort for families from Ajaccio.

ORNANO

Between the Prunelli and Taravo rivers, the mountain mass of the Ornano is the domain of the shepherd, an entirely pastoral region with a proliferation of shepherd villages linked by tracks or roads in poor condition. Sheep and cattle are reared and migrate in winter from the mountains to the lowland at the mouth of the Taravo and around the Gulf of Valinco; some even cross the mountain divide to the eastern coast at Solenzara. In general the economy is declining and the population dwindling, but the western littoral of the Ornano, fronting the Gulf of Ajaccio is the scene of active tourist development. The coastal road from Ajaccio has been improved, water and electricity supplies provided and new holiday residential areas are burgeoning on the unspoilt southern shore of the Gulf of Ajaccio. Thus the Ornano reflects the general trend throughout the island, the forsaking of the mountain and the gravitation to the coast.

THE SARTENAIS

South of a line from the Gulf of Valinco to Solenzara on the east coast lies Corsica's 'deep south', in many ways the part of the island least changed by modern development. Apart from one or two localities, there is a general similarity about the whole of southern Corsica. Most of the upland and plateau is here below 1,000m in altitude. Rainfall is markedly lower than to the north, a result both of the lower relief and the more southerly latitude, and the summer drought is thus particularly intense. As compared with the great gulfs of western Corsica, the coastline here consists of minor indentations and smaller gulfs, many of which nevertheless are scenically very attractive. The most distinctive cultural features of the landscape are the sparsity of population and, everywhere, the evidence of neglect and decay in the use of land.

The exceptions to this generally unspectacular landscape are to be found at the coast, in the towns and in the forests. On the Gulf of Valinco, the miniature port of Propriano, has become a thriving tourist centre. Its initial growth was as the *marine* for Sartène, the port serving the Taravo, Baraci and Rizzanese valleys, and a local fishing port. The commercial port function is now of little significance, but the site on the vast Gulf of Valinco, the attraction of the old town, the fine beaches and the growth of yachting and cruising have transformed Propriano. It now has numerous hotels and holiday camps and at the height of the season is outclassed only by Calvi in terms of tourist animation. Given improvements in communications, the expansion of tourism seems inevitable.

By contrast, Sartène has resisted change and remains more 'Corsican' in character than any other town in the island. The capital of the Sartenais, an area of conservatism and traditionalism, Sartène has always maintained an introspective attitude and until the present century, a closed economy. Here suspicion and mistrust, not only of the outside powers but also between the great clans, have been less broken down. Sartène remains something of an anachronism in Corsica's urban pattern, and the town shows signs of a decline in population. Not so Porto-Vecchio, at the same latitude on the eastern coast. The old town has a fortified hillside site, set in a landscape of olive groves, new farms

50

on reclaimed land, and backed by the cork oak forests which provide the townsfolk with one of their principal activities. A kilometre away from the old town with its remaining Genoese ramparts, the *marine* on the sheltered and narrow Gulf of Porto-Vecchio, combines the functions of commercial and fishing port with a yacht marina. Tourism is expanding on the gulf and with over 5,000 inhabitants Porto-Vecchio is the largest town of the south.

The great forests of the south lie in the eastern part of the Sartenais. The road from Sartène to Solenzara via Zonza and the Col de Bavella is regarded by many as the most beautiful pass in the island, with its superb combination of mountain, forest and vista. From Zonza, another road crosses the mountains to Porto-Vecchio through the Forest of Ospedale which combines the tranquillity of the forest with a splendid view of the whole of the Gulf of Porto-Vecchio.

Corsica reserves its most exotic and individual landscape to the extreme southern tip of the island. South of the Gulf of Santa Manza, the hard crystalline rocks give way to a limestone table-land. The low rainfall combined with porous rock make this the most desiccated part of the island, and only a spare and stunted maquis vegetation, termed *mucchia,* covers the rock. The landscape recalls that of southern Provence rather than Corsica. Overlooking a sheltered gulf to the north and perched on the edge of precipitous cliffs to the south, Bonifacio occupies the most remarkable site in the island. In fact in many ways the tiny region of Bonifacio is separate from the island. The dialect spoken there is peculiar to the region and the inhabitants frequently speak of 'going into Corsica' when they travel from Bonifacio. The town's history has always been influenced by external connections and Sardinia, only twelve kilometres distant, is easily accessible from this southernmost bastion.

3   THE TROUBLED PAST

THE early chapters of Corsica's history as an inhabited island are shrouded in mystery. Comparatively little is known of the initial peopling, but it appears possible that in the tenth millenium BC pastoralists with a megalithic culture entered the island. Evidence of this culture takes the form of simple dolmens, of which the best example is to be found in the south, at Fontanaccia near Sartène. This culture appears to have been supplanted through an incursion of Ligurians, possibly during the middle of the second millenium BC. There followed a pronounced artistic evolution represented by menhirs portraying the human form and frequently aligned in rows, a culture which was in turn replaced in the latter half of the second millenium BC through an invasion of Iberian-Celtic people. These bronze age people have left much more elaborate vestiges, in the form of fortified camps, stone circles, altars and sculptured menhirs. The most impressive buildings they constructed were circular vaulted towers, to which the name *torre* has been applied; hence the term *Torréenne* has come to be given to the culture of the island during this period.

Prehistoric remains, especially dolmens and menhirs, are liberally distributed throughout the island, but the site from which the outlines of the island's prehistory have been deciphered is the camp at Filitosa, to the north of the Gulf of Valinco. Here are represented all three stages of the prehistoric civilisation, the simple dolmens and standing stones, the more elaborate sculptured menhirs, and the complex camps of the Torréenne culture.

Although much remains to be discovered about the prehistory of Corsica, it is established that at the dawn of history the island was inhabited by pastoral groups of Iberian and Celto-Ligurian origin, organised into local clans. The crossroads location of the

Page 53 (above) Sculptured menhirs at the prehistoric site at Filitosa, south-west Corsica; (right) Pisan watchtower at Nonza, Cap Corse

Page 54 (left) Patriot in his capital town—a statue of Paoli in Corte; *(below)* Napoleon Bonaparte's birthplace at Ajaccio

island attracted visits by Phoenician traders, exchanging their goods for the produce of the island. At this time Corsica was thickly wooded and rich in wildlife, but there is no evidence of an attempt at colonisation. The ancient name of the island *Kyrnos* may be derived from the Phoenician word *Kersica*, meaning 'island of promontories'. Alternative origins of the name come from early Greek legends, or from descriptive terms, such as *Korsai*, a forest.

Etymological and other evidence suggests that Corsica had many contacts throughout the Mediterranean at the dawn of history but her entry into the wider scene of Mediterranean history began by incursions, starting in the sixth century BC, of outside groups seeking to establish permanent colonies. This was to become the leit-motif of her troubled history throughout the ensuing two millenia.

GREEKS AND ROMANS

The first Greek incursion occurred in 565 BC when a group of Phocaeans established a base at Alalia, on the eastern plain. Thirty years later they were forced to abandon their settlement after the sea battle of Alalia in which they were defeated by Carthaginians and Etruscans. In 453 BC the Etruscans were in turn driven out by Greeks from Syracuse, who themselves were supplanted by Carthaginians in 280 BC. The impact of these incursions was limited; the settlements were restricted to the littoral, but it is clear that the Greeks introduced a certain cultural influence. To them may be attributed the introduction of writing and, through the creation of Alalia, the first vestige of an urban civilisation. The Greeks also introduced the vine, the olive and cereals, and they prospected the island for minerals. Above all they brought the island into contact with a wider world, a trend which was later intensified by the Roman occupation.

Roman interest in Corsica stemmed from the rivalry with Carthage for domination of the western Mediterranean. This precipitated the capture of Alalia from Carthage in 260 BC and

D

the construction on the same site of the new city of Aleria, as a port, administrative centre and bridgehead for the subjection of Corsica to Roman rule. In fact this process proved to be no easy matter and spanned the century from 260 to 163 BC. The subjection of the island required numerous campaigns, which were interspersed with uneasy truces. The hostilities culminated in 173 BC in a general uprising of the Corsicans and final victory by the Romans was not achieved until 163 BC. By this time, the island had reconciled itself to Roman domination and to becoming incorporated in the most powerful empire in the western world. There followed six centuries of peace until the Vandal invasions during which time the island was administered as an imperial province and some degree of Romanisation was achieved. Apart from its strategic importance, the island was not without economic resources of value to Rome. Resin, wax, honey and charcoal were exploited, while the eastern plain, at this time still free from malaria, produced grain. In the interior the Romans discovered and exploited mineral springs.

The Romans left the pre-existing social system and administrative divisions little disturbed and the indigenous Corsican culture of the interior remained remarkably unchanged by the occupation. Nevertheless, some elements were introduced by the Romans which proved more or less durable. Chief of these was latin speech which was disseminated along the lines of the routes which the Romans established in order to connect the main productive areas of the island. Secondly, the growth of Aleria and the foundation of a second town at Mariana, at the mouth of the Golo, kept alive the urban civilisation introduced by the Greeks. Finally, the spread of Christianity during the second century was perhaps the most effective and far-reaching issue of the Roman occupation. The special attachment of Corsica to the Papacy, throughout the troubled years of the Dark Ages and the anarchy of the medieval period, was the outcome of that Roman endowment.

The collapse of Rome heralded a long period of chaos as the island fell prey to successive barbarian groups. The history of these six centuries of confusion is poorly documented but the general background of oppression, misery and depopulation is clearly established. After 455 the island was invaded in turn by Vandals and Ostrogoths, who exacted tribute from the population, but more widespread pillage and brutality occurred during two centuries of occupation by the Byzantines. In turn, the Byzantines were replaced by Lombards who invaded the island in 725. Their control was short-lived, for in 755 Pépin le Bref, ruler of the Ostrogothic kingdom of Italy, placed the island under the protection of the Papacy—a decision confirmed by Charlemagne in 774. This was far from assuring a respite from further attack. From the eighth to the tenth century Saracen marauders were rampant throughout the western Mediterranean and these moslem pirates pillaged the island until they were ejected for the last time in 1077. In spite of their prolonged incursions, little remains of the era of Saracen control other than the inclusion of a number of words into the language, the introduction of some Saracen place-names and family titles, and the injection of some Saracen blood into the native stream.

PISA VERSUS GENOA

The experience of six centuries of domination by the barbarians did little to diminish the innate tendency of the Corsican people towards internecine warfare. On the contrary, the departure of the Saracens ushered in a period of feudal anarchy within the island in which warfare between rival lords attained extreme violence. Symptomatic of the atrocities of the times was the fate of Arrigo Bel Messere (Henri le Beau Sire), an enlightened leader whose reward for attempting to restore justice to the island was assassination and the drowning of his seven children in the year 1000. In desperation as a result of the arbitrary and harsh treatment meted out by the feudal lords, the war-sick populace turned yet again to the Papacy for arbitration between the conflicting factions.

The struggle between the powerful Cinarchese seigneurs of

the Au-delà des Monts, and the counts of Biancolacci, which caused widespread death and destruction, was typical of these feudal conflicts. In response to the pleas of the Corsican people Pope Gregory VII appointed Landolphe, archbishop of Pisa, to administer the island and, by conferring the same task upon the succession to the archbishopric, effectively transferred control of the island to Pisa. The Pisan period, the twelfth and thirteenth centuries, was marked by a return to relative calm, during which the agricultural area was extended and public works, bridges and churches were constructed. The Pisan churches are particularly fine monuments of this relatively peaceful interlude in Corsican history.

The progress made under the aegis of Pisa was not to remain unimpeded. Pisan control was not only uncertain in the Au-delà des Monts but was also contested in the north of the island by the Genoese, who had retained a foothold in Cap Corse since the time of the crusades against the Saracens. It was inevitable that the political rivalry between the republics of Genoa and Pisa should be extended to confrontation over the control of Corsica. Once more the island looked to the Papacy for mediation and on this occasion an attempt at a compromise was made by Pope Innocent II. In 1133 he divided the island into six bishoprics, allocating the three northern dioceses, Mariana, Nebbio and Accia to Genoa, and the southern dioceses of Ajaccio, Sagone and Aleria to Pisa. This compromise satisfied neither contestant. In the conflict that followed, Bonifacio, a town with a strategic location changed hands several times before falling permanently under Genoese control after a surprise attack in 1195. The Corsicans were expelled from the town and a Genoese colony was established there.

In 1278, the Genoese secured control of the northern approaches to the island by occupying Calvi and transforming it into an impregnable fortress. By introducing Genoese settlers and by according generous privileges to the townsfolk, Genoa was able to retain the loyalty of Calvi throughout the various reverses which marked the republic's control of the island. The demise of Pisa was finally sealed by the Genoese victory in the naval battle of Meloria, off the coast of Tuscany in 1284. The protracted struggle between Genoa and Pisa encouraged the divisive forces at work in the island. The feudal lords were courted by the two republics and changed their allegiance whenever it seemed to be to their advantage. The most remarkable volte-face was that of Sinucello della Rocca, one of the island's popular leaders and now a legendary folk hero. After first siding with the Genoese, he later disputed their control of Bonifacio and in defeat sought refuge in Pisa in 1280. Supported by the Pisans he returned to Corsica to resume the struggle against Genoa. After the Genoese naval victory of Meloria he simulated an understanding with them in 1289, only to rise against them again in 1290, claiming leadership of the island. He called a *consulte*, a general assembly of leaders, at Mariana, and promulgated an enlightened constitution involving the rule of law and taxation proportionate to wealth. In defiance of the Genoese presence on the island in their fortified citadelles, the assembly regarded the island as being independent though under the nominal tutelage of Pisa.

The magnanimity of the concepts of his constitution earned Sinucello the popular title of *Giudice de Cinarca*, the judge of the Cinarca, but his ideals were to be short-lived. He was unable to suppress jealousy and mistrust between the rival clans, and his tendency to change sides apparently more through opportunism than conviction earned him many enemies even within his own family. In 1299, reconciliation between Genoa and Pisa led to his banishment, and in spite of a renewed struggle he was eventually betrayed by his own son and transported infirm and blind to Genoa where he died in 1306 at the age of 98. Ephemeral though his influence seems to have been when viewed against the centuries of turbulent history, Sinucello stands out as the prototype of the many legendary figures who cross the stage of Corsican history—half heroic, half tragic; part patriot, part opportunist and adventurer. With the collapse of Sinucello's movement, opposition to Genoa diminished and in 1347, another *consulte* of barons and seigneurs voted to accept Genoese control.

Although the Genoese domination continued after these events until 1768 its effectiveness was never total. Since Genoa was preoccupied initially with a struggle for power in the eastern Mediterranean, especially against Venice, Corsica held for the republic more strategic than economic or colonial value. Control of Corsica was the key to control of the trade routes of the Ligurian Sea, which were contested with Pisa. The essential basis of strategic control, both within and without the island was the chain of citadelle towns that Genoa created between 1195 and 1539—Calvi, St Florent, Bastia, Porto-Vecchio, Bonifacio and Ajaccio. Complete political control of the interior was never fully attained, nor did Genoa succeed in suppressing the traditional hostility between the populace and the feudal seigneurs or the rivalry between the clans. These conditions of domestic anarchy were excellent breeding ground for the growth of internal opposition to the Genoese overlords and also caused other foreign powers to take an interest in the island. At the same time the persistence of rivalry and mistrust prevented the formation of an island force sufficiently strong and united to expel the Genoese.

From this confused background there emerged about the middle of the fourteenth century the *Terre des Communes*, a popular uprising against the excesses of the seigneurs, motivated by a search for freedom from feudal tyranny. In the course of this quest many of the feudal castles were demolished. The movement was strongest in the En-deça des Monts; the Au-delà des Monts remained the *Terre des Seigneurs*. The democratic and communal spirit of the movement was inspired by similar ventures in northern Italy and was associated in Corsica with the name of Sambucuccio d'Alando, the chief of the Communes. The movement was based on the grouping of communes or parishes into *pièves*. Each commune had as its leader a *podestat* who was aided by two *anziani*, all three offices being filled by popular election with universal suffrage. The podestat and his 'ancients' headed a communal council consisting of all the village artisans, each of whom had been elected.

The essential feature of the movement was the communal ownership of land. Arable land was leased to individuals to farm in their own right while the pastoral land was open to communal grazing. Unfortunately, this early attempt to achieve a just and democratic society was short-lived. Internal dissension and indifference on the part of Genoa weakened the initial impetus of the system and thus the seigneurs were able to continue to indulge in oppression which Genoa was powerless to restrain. The indifference of Genoa to the island's affairs resulted from her continuing preoccupation with the struggle against Venice, and in 1378 the republic delegated the task of exploiting Corsica to a syndicate of business interests, the *Maona*. This syndicate hired troops and built a fortress at Bastia in 1380 as a base for their commercial activities.

Vincentello d'Istria

While Genoa was distracted by her rivalry with other Mediterranean city states, a contender for the island's sovereignty appeared on the scene. The Pope had, in 1296, nominally ceded the island to the Kingdom of Aragon. With the growing importance of Barcelona in the fifteenth century, King Alphonse V judged the moment ripe to establish Aragon's claim to the island on which Genoa held such a tenuous grip. He enlisted the aid of a Corsican nobleman brought up in the court of Aragon, Vincentello d'Istria, Count of the Cinarca, and an implacable enemy of Genoa. In campaigns in 1407 and 1408, Vincentello raised widespread revolt against the Genoese, captured Bastia and assumed the title of Count of Corsica. In 1418, the King of Aragon nominated Vincentello Viceroy of Corsica and mounted a further attempt to rid the island of the Genoese. Bastia was recaptured and the Genoese were driven from all their strongholds except Calvi and Bonifacio.

Two years later Alphonse joined the struggle personally in support of Vincentello. Calvi capitulated and the whole island acknowledged Aragonese sovereignty with the exception of the beleaguered Genoese bridgehead of Bonifacio. For the next thirteen years Vincentello reigned as Viceroy from the stronghold that he built at Corte in 1420. During these years, however, the interest of Aragon waned, as Alponse V embarked on the conquest of Naples. In spite of an attempt at enlightened rule, Vincentello ran into opposition, initially from the seigneurs but eventually from popular uprisings. He was obliged to seek refuge in Florence and while attempting to return to Spain in 1434, he was captured at sea off Bastia, handed over to the Genoese and decapitated. With the death of Vincentello an opportunity for a united island under a patriotic leader evaporated as Corsica once more lapsed into anarchy.

Beset by struggles against the Turks and Venice, Genoa again turned to private interests to administer the troublesome island, and this time delegated the task to the Bank of St George in 1453. This proved unacceptable to several of the leading seigneurs and a period of chaos ensued, marked by atrocities, betrayals, bloodthirsty reprisals and a general breakdown of coherent rule. The situation was further complicated by the fact that in 1463, Genoa fell under the control of the Duke of Milan and the Bank of St George ceded its rights in Corsica to this new master. Relative peace reigned in the island for a decade, but the rapacity of the governors installed by the Duke of Milan, further incitement by Aragon and the habitual internal rivalries between the seigneurs brought a renewal of conflict. In 1476, Genoa threw off Milanese domination and was once more ready to assume control of Corsica.

A bitter war was launched in 1485 against the seigneurs of the Au-delà which was marked by unbelievable atrocity on both sides. After twenty years of fighting, the noble families had been decimated, the whole island suffered economic ruin and a series of outbreaks of the plague had occurred. Despairing of any future in their war-torn island, many young Corsicans emigrated to find their fortunes in Europe. Here they found employment as mercenary soldiers—a career for which their vocation and talent was scarcely to be doubted. The murderous battles and ensuing extermination of the leading seigneurs brought the island firmly under Genoese control and sounded the death knell of feudal power. Although the family names continued and lost none of their significance in terms of traditional loyalties and rivalries, the political power of the seigneurs was at last extinguished. In the future, the population increasingly looked beyond the island for aid in the struggle against Genoa, rather than to its erstwhile noble tyrants.

The career of Sampiero Corso

One son of Corsica who emigrated to serve as a mercenary played a major role in the island's history. This was Sampiero Corso, born in 1498 in the heart of the Au-delà des Monts. After serving in a variety of mercenary armies Sampiero became colonel-in-chief of the Corsican regiment of Francis I of France and distinguished himself as a leader in the struggle between France and Austria, Genoa having taken the side of Austria. The Treaty of Crespy in 1544 interrupted the war and enabled Sampiero to return to Corsica where he married Vannina, a daughter of the powerful seigneurial family, the Ornano. His prestige made Sampiero a natural focus of opposition to the Genoese who reacted by imprisoning him. The intervention of Francis I secured his release and he returned to France more than ever determined to settle his account with Genoa.

The opportunity was soon offered as war between France and Austria broke out again in 1551, with Genoa once more allied with Charles V of Austria. With the help of their Turkish allies, the French pursued vigorous campaigns in Corsica, driving the Genoese back into their citadelles at St Florent and Calvi. Sampiero won noble victories but gradually lost the confidence of the French and even of his natural allies, the Ornano family. In 1555 he was recalled to France and in the following year the Corsicans requested Henry II of France to annex the island.

Henry agreed with enthusiasm, but Corsica was to remain French only briefly, for in the peace settlement of Cateau-Cambrésis which ended the war between Austria and France in 1559, Corsica was returned once more to the despised Genoese.

For four short years the Corsicans had appreciated their attachment to France, with its liberal quality and promise of a more settled future. By contrast, the Genoese redoubled their efforts to suppress and systematically exploit the island. Frustrated in his ambition for a French Corsica, Sampiero was by no means reconciled to accepting Genoese control. On the contrary he travelled far and wide in Europe and North Africa in search of support to liberate the island, even to the extent of visiting the Sultan at Constantinople to request the support of the Ottoman fleet. During this journey a further drama unfolded, for the Genoese made peace offers to Sampiero's wife, Vannina d'Ornano. She attempted to travel to Genoa but was detained at Antibes and imprisoned near Marseilles. Hearing of this interlude and believing himself betrayed, Sampiero himself strangled Vannina despite her pleas of innocence.

Despairing of substantial outside help, Sampiero landed in the Gulf of Valinco with a small band in 1564. He rallied support and unleashed a bitter war against the Genoese. After three years of terrible fighting, Sampiero remained undefeated and his fall in 1567 was only brought about by treason, when one of his comrades, Vittolo, accompanied by members of the Ornano family who sought revenge for the death of Vannina, led him into an ambush. So died one of the most colourful figures in Corsican history. A patriot and hero, implacable in his hatred of Genoese domination, his career finished on a note of tragedy with the death of Vannina and his own betrayal. His life was not without lasting significance however, for it brought about direct French involvement in Corsican affairs.

The century of iron

Exhausted by the conflicts and warfare that had continued with little interruption since the Vandal invasions of the fifth century, the Corsicans were unable to resist the Genoese masters any longer. Sensing this lassitude the new governor issued a generous amnesty and in 1571 published a legal code, the *Statuti Civili e Criminali*. A semblance of democracy and autonomy was instituted, but true power still remained the prerogative of the resident Genoese administrators. Although open warfare subsided, the whole of the seventeenth century was marked by misery and suffering which earned it the title of 'the century of iron' Agriculture and trade suffered under excessive taxation, intermittent famines, epidemics, and Saracen raids further depleted the population, which had already dwindled through emigration.

The bitterness of the people mounted steadily. Amongst their specific grievances was the planting by Genoa of a Greek colony, composed of refugees from Islam, at Paomia on the Gulf of Sagone in 1676. Genoese exploitation of the island intensified in proportion to her decline in the face of the political and economic rise of Spain, France, and Britain. The Genoese administrators on the island acquired considerable freedom to practise abuse, particularly in the matter of taxation. Lack of real autonomy, excessive taxation and the reluctance of the Genoese to accept the traditional status of the leaders of the great families were the main factors in the growing atmosphere of revolt. The opposition finally burst into open revolt in 1729, when the villages in the *piève* of Bozio refused to pay taxes demanded by the governor of Corte. The war of independence had begun.

THE WAR OF INDEPENDENCE

The uprising against Genoa spread rapidly through the island as a popular movement rather than as an organised and coherent campaign. Many of the nobility were desirous more of winning concessions than of achieving total secession. The hostilities thus had a guerilla character and did not assume the character of a national war until, after strenuous Genoese reprisals, a *consulte* of patriots held in Corte in 1731 agreed on concerted action, which received the approval of eminent churchmen.

From the outset it was obvious that whatever the specific outcome of the struggle, there was little hope for an island of little more than 100,000 inhabitants, bitterly divided in all but hatred of Genoa, to maintain independence for long. A subsidiary of the war of independence therefore became the question of which great power would fill the vacuum if Genoa should be defeated. Genoa appealed for help to the Emperor of Austria, but the imperial troops were forced by the strength of the Corsican opposition to conclude a peace treaty with the rebels in 1732 at Corte. The following year an independent Corsican government was proclaimed to which the Genoese riposted by blockading the island. There next occurred a bizarre incident, scarcely credible except in the context of an island grown accustomed to practically every turn of fate.

In 1736 an English vessel arrived at Aleria, loaded with arms and food supplies, from which disembarked Théodore de Neuhoff, an adventurer who had frequented the courts of Europe. He had met Corsican exiles in Tuscany and imagined it his destiny to rule the island. Impressed by his lavish dress, apparent wealth and connections with the great powers, the Corsicans succumbed to his outrageous claim to be king of the island. His election as king was confirmed at a ceremony at the convent of Alesani and immediately he surrounded himself with the trappings of a constitutional monarch, King Théodore I of Corsica. He formed a legislative assembly, distributed various honorary titles and even had coins struck bearing his head. However, his promises failed to materialise, his troops suffered defeat at Bastia, promised reinforcements failed to appear and his supposed influence with the great powers was seen to be a fiction. His unpopularity was such that he quickly delegated his powers to a regency council and scarcely seven months after his arrival he made an ignominious departure from the tiny port of Solenzara.

Bereft of their ephemeral monarchy, the Corsicans continued their struggle for independence. It became increasingly clear that Genoa's hold on the island could not be maintained. The question of a successor became of immediate importance and Genoa now appealed to France for aid. France collaborated, though more with a view to acquiring the island in the long term than to obliging the enfeebled Genoese. The French achieved pacification of the island and attempted a reconciliation between Corsica and Genoa under their own guarantee. Not surprisingly, the Corsicans were reluctant to credit Genoa with good intentions and the revolt continued.

Once more the great powers, now divided into two blocks after the Treaty of Worms, intervened. Britain, Spain and Sardinia espoused the cause of Corsica while Genoa again turned to France. In 1747 French troops landed in Corsica, as much in opposition to British aspirations as to give assistance to Genoa. The French leader, the Marquis de Cursay, acted as an *intendant* and gained the widespread respect of the Corsicans by his firm but impartial application of justice. Although technically controlling Corsica on behalf of the Genoese, de Cursay identified himself more with the islander's cause, making personal friends with their leading patriot Gaffori. The Genoese subsequently succeeded in having the French army evacuated from the island, but there was no longer any question of re-establishing their own control. Having experienced the enlightened rule of de Cursay, the people were determined to be either part of France or totally independent. Yet again warfare against the Genoese continued under Gaffori until his assassination brought to the fore a new leader who was destined to play a decisive role in the island's destiny.

Pascal Paoli, patriot

Of all Corsican heroes, perhaps Paoli comes closest to the pure patriot—steadfast in his pursuit of power certainly, but motivated more by concern for his people than by the sterile clan rivalry. Above all he exercised power constructively and creatively rather than in settlement of scores or in self-enrichment.

Brought up in exile at Naples, where he distinguished himself as a soldier, Paoli landed in Corsica in 1755 at the age of twenty-eight, and was proclaimed 'General of the Nation'. He established a new constitution containing provision for the election of representatives, reduced taxation and created schools and, in his capital Corte, a university. Economic life was revived, political unity was gradually restored, and Paoli's reputation as a civilised statesman spread across Europe. His efforts to renew the island's life were remarkable. He encouraged agriculture, the draining of marshes and the construction of roads and bridges. At l'Ile Rousse on the coast of Balagne he founded a new port from which to bypass the blockade run by the Genoese from their citadelle ports.

Genoa made a last appeal to France and in 1756 French garrisons occupied Ajaccio, Calvi and St Florent. Twelve years later Genoa bowed before the inevitable and conceded ownership of the island to France. After four centuries the domination of Genoa had been thrown off—but independence was not yet achieved for an accommodation now had to be found with France.

Paoli admired France and immediately appealed for recognition of the island's independence under French protection. This appeal was rejected and Paoli's army was soundly defeated in May 1769 at Ponte Nuovo. On 15 August of that year, the very day on which Napoleon was born, Corsica was proclaimed French. Paoli fled to England, where he was held in great esteem throughout his exile. The outbreak of the French revolution saw the recall of Paoli to France at the request of the National Assembly. He was appointed a lieutenant-general and given the command of Corsica in 1790.

This might have seemed a fitting end to a remarkable career, being returned to his own people as the champion of their freedom by a government representing a revolution of the people of France. In fact, after a very brief period, Paoli became increasingly estranged from the development of the revolution. The death of Louis XVI and the political and religious intolerance were distasteful to a man with deep respect for civilisation and enlightenment. Intrigue against him grew in the General Assembly at Paris and after the failure of an expedition he led against Sardinia he was summoned to Paris to give an account of himself.

Paoli refused to submit to this humiliation, declared the secession of the island, raised a militia and called upon Admiral Hood, in charge of the British Fleet blockading Toulon, for assistance. The French opposition was overcome and the British fleet captured Bastia, St Florent and Calvi in 1794; it was in the siege of Calvi that Nelson lost his left eye. At this point Paoli convoked a *consulte* which declared Corsica free of the Revolutionary Convention government of France. The relations between Britain and Corsica were, however, ill defined and marked on Paoli's side by mistrust. British interest lay chiefly in the short-term political demands of the war against France rather than in the desire to assume the role of protector of the island for an indefinite period. A British governor, Sir Gilbert Eliot, was installed in 1794, but was soon overwhelmed by would-be Corsican aspirants to power and privilege. Disappointed in the attitude of his British allies, Paoli once more chose exile in England where he died in 1807. His body, first entombed in Westminster Abbey, was later moved to his native village of Morosaglia in the Castagniccia. With the exile of Paoli, British popularity waned in direct proportion to the growing prestige of Napoleon, a son of Corsica, during his Italian campaign. In 1796, the last British forces sailed from Bonifacio, and with the return of Corsica to France, the separate political history of the island was virtually concluded. During the Napoleonic regime, Corsica was administered by military rule, Napoleon understanding only too well the propensity of his countrymen for anarchy if given too remote an administration. After the Restoration, Corsica became and has since remained a *département* of France, undifferentiated from those of the mainland, and has retained this status ever since.

FRENCH CORSICA

With political and administrative integration into France, the history of Corsica became tied to that of the French nation as a whole, though it has had its own peculiarities. Corsica's pride in the attachment to France has been poorly reciprocated by state action on behalf of the island. The nineteenth century was one of general neglect, with occasional small-scale and half-hearted measures of aid. Although regular shipping services were established from Marseilles in 1832, the railway link between Bastia and Ajaccio was not completed until 1894. Although Corsican loyalty was reaffirmed by full participation in the French forces during the Franco-Prussian War and the first World War, little was done in return to check the degeneration of the economy and the decline in population that have been the most significant features of the island in the past hundred years.

The apparent indifference of the French government to the fate of the island was a major element in the attempt made by the Italian Fascist movement to gain a foothold there. This attempt began on a subtle note after 1918 through the medium of propaganda. Fascist support was given to the insignificant Corsican 'autonomy' movement, exploiting its newspapers to glorify the achievements of the Duce and to accuse the French of neglecting the island. Scholarships were offered to young Corsicans for study at Italian universities, and a stream of historical, linguistic and scientific studies of the island were published in Italy, giving an appearance of respectability to the Italian interest in the island. An attempt was even made to rehabilitate the Genoese occupation in order to justify the argument that Corsica should naturally be part of Italy. This insidious propaganda had little or no impact on Corsicans, who lost no opportunity to proclaim their loyalty to France. By the outbreak of the second World War, the objective of Fascist propaganda—to create a favourable social and political atmosphere for annexation by diplomacy or conquest—was unachieved. With the fall of France, German and Italian commissions were established on the island but passive patriotic demonstrations left no doubt where the island's sympathies lay. In November 1942 an Italian squadron landed at Bastia and a full-scale occupation began. At its maximum extent, the occupation consisted of 80,000 Italian and 10,000 German troops. As on the mainland, the occupation began tactfully but soon deteriorated into a harsh repression by the

Page 71 View westwards across the eastern plain, with a modern irrigation reservoir

Page 72 Land reclamation on the eastern plains: *(above)* bulldozing *maquis* for new farm land; *(below)* ploughing reclaimed land

military and by the *Ovra*, the Italian secret police. Shootings, torture and deportation were the methods by which resistance was repressed.

Contact was nevertheless maintained with Free France. In April 1941 Fred Scamaroni, an agent sent by de Gaulle, committed suicide rather than risk revealing information under torture. By his patriotism he became the symbol of a growing resistance movement which, taking refuge among the island's maquis, gave a new title to the French underground movement as a whole. The *maquisards* were supplied with arms by submarine from Algeria and by air drops by the RAF and the Italian capitulation in September 1943 was greeted by an armed uprising of over 10,000 patriots. Armoured reinforcements arrived from North Africa and General Giraud was appointed commander of the operations to liberate the island. The Italian troops were quickly forced into aligning with the partisans against the German troops, now swollen by contingents driven out of Sardinia and using Bastia as a point of embarkation for the mainland. Fierce fighting developed in the Sartenais and on the eastern coastal plain, where the railway line was demolished. The campaign reached its climax at the end of September in fierce fighting in the Col de Teghime and the approaches to Bastia. Bombed first by the Germans and then by the Allies, Bastia suffered a great deal of damage. By 4 October 1943 the German resistance had been extinguished, and Corsica became the first *département* of France to celebrate its liberation.

4   THE CORSICAN PROBLEM

THE turbulent political history of Corsica has inevitably
exacted a social and economic price which the island continues to pay. While the island economy remained largely
self-supporting, the upheaval caused by warfare was short term
in effect. Thus population numbers had a tendency to oscillate :
periods of war, anarchy, famine, and plague produced serious
economic disruption and corresponding depopulation; the inter-
ludes of peace gave an opportunity for the population balance
to be restored. This pattern of fluctuation, with an overall tendency for the population to grow, extended throughout the centuries of Genoese occupation. With the return to relative calm
after the French annexation in 1789, the population appears to
have doubled in the following century reaching a total of approximately 280,000 in 1880. This is probably the highest total population achieved by the island.

The present population may be generously estimated at 180,000
inhabitants. In the space of less than a century, the island has
lost 100,000 inhabitants, over a third of its total since the year
of maximum population. As the towns have continued to grow,
this implies that rural Corsica has lost over half of its population
since 1880. In simple terms this decline represents the emigration,
particularly of young people, from an island which no longer
offered economic security once it was exposed to modern commercial conditions. Specifically the Corsican exodus reflects the
catastrophic decay of the traditional agricultural economy and
the failure to provide alternative employment.

Corsica has been likened to a beautiful body progressively
becoming senile. The flow of emigrants has been termed a
haemorrhage, a bleeding of the vital force of the island, its young

74

people. It is common to speak of 'the Corsican Problem', a global phrase that embraces the many ailments that account for the present retarded development of the island. The perceptive visitor who ventures away from the popular tourist enclaves is soon confronted with massive evidence of decay in the rural landscape. This other Corsica is in most respects the real Corsica, of abandoned fields, of half-deserted villages, where the island's modern economic and social drama is being enacted.

THE MOUNTAIN—CRADLE OF THE TRADITIONAL ECONOMY

It seems likely that early in the island's history the coastal plains of Corsica were more densely populated than at present. Descriptions of the Plain of Aleria as a Roman granary are no doubt exaggerated but archaeological evidence, particularly of the large number of anchorages, suggests that these lowlands were widely used in those early times. Under the stimulus of the Pax Romana, the eastern coastal plain was cultivated for cereals—the working of the land checking the development of swampy breeding grounds for malaria. The collapse of Rome and the ensuing barbarian invasions drove the population to abandon the plains for the safety of the mountains and forests, and the lowlands became infested with malaria and uninhabitable at the height of summer. To the problems of disease was added the perennial hazard of exposure to outside attack, and the plains were to remain virtually empty for centuries. The essential features of the traditional economy were therefore developed in a mountain setting. Isolated in those early days by poor communications and hampered by incessant warfare, it was natural that the Corsicans should seek to exploit their mountain environment in a self-sufficient way.

On the lower hill slopes and better soils a society of agriculturalists evolved, growing cereals as staple crops and supplementing them with vines, fruit and chestnuts. Combined with poultry and domestic animals this economy provided sustenance for the

75

hilltop villages. Some migration in the spring, before the malaria season, to plant quick-growing crops on the plains was also practised. On the higher slopes and throughout most of the Au-delà des Monts, herding livestock was the chief means of livelihood, the shepherds grazing their sheep and goats on high mountain pastures in summer and migrating to the coast for winter pasture. The co-existence of pastoral and sedentary agriculture was at times uneasy, with frequent disputes over land and water resources.

In more favourable areas, such as the Balagne and the Castagniccia, these forms of traditional agriculture were able to support quite a dense network of villages. In the Castagniccia, the planting of huge chestnut groves created a useful multi-purpose resource, yielding flour and animal feed, tannin and timber. In the chain of tiny coves backed by well-drained valleys in Cap Corse agriculture could be combined with fishing. The pastoral system of the interior mountains was never able to support such high population densities as did crop farming for it needed a great deal of land to support and employ an individual family.

Although the terrain was difficult the natural resources of the mountains were by no means negligible. Under the Genoese, a considerable amount of forest clearing and hill-slope terracing was achieved in Cap Corse and throughout the En-deçà des Monts, so that cereal cultivation could be carried on high up the mountain sides. Given peaceful conditions there is no reason to suppose that a stable economy could not have been achieved, based on the exchange of animal and crop produce. Sadly the peace, which would have permitted the draining and irrigation of the valleys and the development of artisan industries, was all too rarely present and in consequence the economy atrophied in its traditional form. Although under Genoese exploitation substantial amounts of Corsican produce, notably wine, chestnut flour, olives and cedrats, found their way into foreign trade, there was no accompanying investment in agricultural improvement. Heavy taxation by the Genoese and the depredations of war nullified much of the effort. The Corsicans were disinclined to communal effort when this involved reaching agreements between rival clans over the use of land and water and the periods of peace seldom yielded the benefit of co-operative effort. Until the seventeenth century, it is unlikely that the total population exceeded 100,000 inhabitants. Indeed fragmentary records indicate that the periodic famines and plagues produced catastrophic declines in the population, to which must be added the losses due to pirate attacks and resistance to the Genoese, while banditry and the vendetta accounted for as many as 2,000 deaths per annum at the end of the sixteenth century. At the time of the French annexation a total of 110,000 inhabitants seems a reasonable estimate of the population.

NINETEENTH-CENTURY EXPANSION

With political attachment to France, population growth assumed unprecedented proportions. In the century after 1789, the population of Corsica more than doubled to approximately 280,000 in 1880. Several reasons account for this abrupt diversion from past trends. Paramount was the return of political stability. The population of Corsica had always been fertile, but the appearance of large families was offset by premature death by disease, famine or combat, and further reduced by emigration of young men to join the armies of the mainland. Political stability brought with it peace and favourable conditions in which to step up agricultural output. Initially the government did little in a positive sense. Under the governments of Louis XV and Louis XVI, the *Plan Terrier*, an inventory of the island's resources, was drawn up and it was clear that Corsica would yield little for France without a massive drain on the budget for development works. Under the Revolution, the First Empire, and the Restoration Monarchy, symbolic gestures of nominal aid were all that Corsica received.

The revival of population growth in the first part of the nineteenth century was based on a continuation of the traditional farming economy, but set against a background of peace and still protected by insularity from competition with foreign imports. Settled conditions permitted an increase in population and the output of agriculture increased to meet this demand. The Miot Acts of 1801, which suppressed direct taxation and substituted customs duties, aided this general improvement.

Under the Second Empire some direct assistance was given for development works, especially the draining of the smaller lowland plains and the improvement of roads, and for education. By 1880 Corsica reached its zenith in terms of total population and the expansion of agriculture but little innovation had occurred in agriculture beyond some attempt to control indiscriminate grazing in the forests. In 1880 there was little sign of anything resembling industry and artisan crafts had fossilised and were restricted to the production of simple utensils and farming equipment. It was this failure to develop beyond the traditional methods of production with archaic systems of land tenure, the failure to put to use the tens of thousands of hectares of fertile lowland and to create embryonic industries, which was to lay Corsica open to attack by new economic forces which she was powerless to resist.

THE EXODUS

The second half of the nineteenth century initiated the gradual breakdown of the traditional economy and a resultant exodus of population from the island. This collapse is to be attributed to improvements in communications with the mainland, which undermined the island's natural insulation from outside commercial competition. Steamship services had connected Corsica with the mainland since 1828 and by the latter half of the century they were bringing in increasing quantities of foodstuffs and consumer goods. Enfeebled by its archaic structure and lethargic development, Corsican agriculture was unable to compete with the import of low-cost grain. The artisan industries were similarly at a disadvantage in competition with better-quality and lower-priced goods produced by factory methods on the mainland. In the increasingly competitive markets of Europe, Corsica's export outlets fell to more efficient mainland producers who were unhindered by the cost of sea transport. The island's exports of olives declined, and the once extensive cedrat plantations were abandoned. The importing of grain reduced the internal demand for chestnut flour and exports of this commodity ceased.

Not only did improved transport open the gates for imports; it also gave an impetus to one of Corsica's traditional exports, her people, and particularly her young. The basis of the Corsican diaspora was thus an inflow of food and manufactured goods, and an exodus of migrants seeking wider opportunities outside the island. Improvements in education had the effect of training Corsicans beyond the levels of opportunity available on the island and at the same time revealed to them the superior opportunities in metropolitan France and the expanding Empire. By the turn of the century, Corsicans in their thousands were finding careers in civil and colonial service, in the police and in the army. Apart from giving the opportunity to break out from the narrow confines of village life, these careers carried the attraction of early retirement on substantial pensions.

Faced with this desertion, Corsica failed to create the industrial and commercial activities which alone could have checked the exodus. The island had no substantial resources of minerals or fuels and the generation of hydro-electric power could be developed only through massive investment in remote and difficult sites. The cost of importing raw materials and of transporting finished goods deterred all but small-scale manufacturing.

Many ancillary factors added to the decline of both economy and population. Phylloxera destroyed vineyards after 1880, and ink disease attacked the chestnut groves. The growth of the Empire distracted the attention of the government and diverted state and private capital elsewhere. The Franco-Prussian War of 1870, in which 30,000 Corsicans participated, and the first World War deprived the island of population through conscription. For the soldiers who left the island and lived eventful lives, a return to the restricted possibilities of Corsica had little appeal. Moreover the Corsicans may be accused of a certain lethargy in their attitude towards the development of their island : political rivalry and corruption absorbed energies which might otherwise have been used more creatively.

Emigrant citizens of Corsican origin are to be found throughout the former French Empire but the two major centres for them were traditionally the coast of Provence and the Riviera, and Algeria. At the end of the 1960s there were probably 100,000 persons of Corsican descent living in Marseilles—in many ways the true modern capital of the island. As many again were resident in Algeria before independence was granted, which accounted for the widespread sympathy felt in the island for the Generals' Revolt in June 1958. Corsicans migrated less happily away from the climate and slow pace of life of the Mediterranean fringe, but a colony of over 10,000 exists in Paris. The magnitude of the 'diaspora' can be judged from the fact that there are more people of Corsican origin living outside than dwelling on the island.

THE CONSEQUENCES OF DEPOPULATION

The most obvious consequence of the exodus from the island is depopulation on a massive scale, a virtual emptying of the island. From the maximum population of 280,000 in 1880, the total had dropped to 245,000 in 1901 and approximately 180,000 by 1962, The official census figures, which show a total of 275,000 inhabitants in 1962, are entirely bogus. All the census enumerations made this century are gross exaggerations of the true population. In an attempt to gain greater financial resources from the government the practice by the mayors of communes of falsifying census returns has been widespread. Even today, the exact population of the island is uncertain and can only be estimated, but it is highly probable that since 1880 the number of inhabitants has declined by at least 100,000. This decline has been exclusively a rural phenomenon and it may be estimated that during the past half century the rural population has been halved. When it is realised that much of the remaining rural population is elderly it can be appreciated that the population actively engaged in agriculture has declined by much more than 50 per cent. Since the vast majority of emigrants left the island in their youth, the rural population as a whole has become progressively more elderly, the birth rate has declined, and the possibility of replacing the generations of migrants has vanished.

There are approximately 1,300 marriages each year in the island, 2,900 births and 2,300 deaths. The natural increase of only 600 is all too easily offset by emigration. The distortion of the age structure brought about by past depopulation and present-day emigration of young people inevitably influences marriage prospects for young people within the island. It is difficult to summarise this problem because of the absence of adequate data and the contrasts which exist between the towns and the countryside. The situation is further complicated by the fact that the need to leave the island for higher education and, in the case of males, for military service, has enabled many Corsicans to find marriage partners outside the island but does not necessarily result in a permanent absence from the island.

The age structure and male-female ratio is relatively balanced in the main towns, and diverse opportunities exist for meeting suitable marriage partners. The situation is very different in the countryside where in many small villages the unmarried adult population is limited to a mere dozen or so individuals. In these circumstances, the opportunities for marriage are very restricted, especially as a predominance of females is usual. For this reason, and because the formalities and conventions of introduction and courtship are more firmly adhered to than in the towns, the age of marriage tends to be later. In many villages, only one or two marriages take place each year.

Associated with depopulation has been the abandonment of land on a huge scale. Bereft of its labour force agriculture inevitably contracted both in area and in output. The abandonment of the cereal fields that were created painstakingly by terracing steep mountain slopes was inevitable once cheaper imported grain was available, but the degeneration extends beyond this. Without the labour needed for harvesting, the chestnut and olive groves have decayed and output is insignificant. The arable area declined from 37 per cent of the island's land area in 1913 to less than 5 per cent in 1960. The decline in cultivated land has been matched by an inverse advance in the area under maquis scrub, which now covers almost three-quarters of the island. In contrast, using smaller amounts of labour and with a guaranteed outlet for ewe's milk for the production of Roquefort cheese, pastoral farming was better able to resist the consequences of depopulation. From having a virtually self-sufficient economy, the island now has to import over half of its food requirements, despite its much smaller population.

Abandoned by the younger, better educated and more progressive elements of the population, the countryside is a stronghold of traditional and conservative attitudes, resistant to change and rarely capable of innovation. This inevitably acts as a barrier to improvements, particularly of land tenure, for the peasant has little interest in reforms which he mistrusts, particularly when he is of an age not to expect to live long enough to benefit from the results. Such apathy precludes the introduction of the radical and long-term reforms which alone can offer hope of recovery.

The dwindling village populations and the ageing of the inhabitants have increased the isolation and the sense of desolation of much of rural Corsica. In many villages half of the houses are abandoned and falling into ruins, and the number of shops and services has declined. The abiding impression left with the visitor must be the aura of physical decay which prevails in the Corsican landscape. This is not to suggest that rural depopulation has gravely disfigured the island. The appearance of chestnut and olive groves changes little with their abandonment, the rampant maquis adds rich tints to the landscape, the hilltop villages lose none of the majesty of their site for being half empty. Nevertheless, the evidence of degeneration intrudes into the landscape immediately one leaves the principal towns. The reality of a decadent economy and of the decline of a proud rural society is inescapable, in spite of the natural beauty of the landscape. Corsica must now be considered as an underdeveloped island. While other Mediterranean islands have witnessed great increases in population during the last hundred years and, since 1945, have experienced impressive economic development, Corsica experienced unmitigated decline until the 1960s. The exodus of its people is both a cause and a consequence of the lack of development. As the economy decayed so people left, and as people left so the task of development became more difficult. The diaspora is therefore the kernel of the 'Corsican Problem', and the image of the island as a dying body is by no means extravagant. Certain attributes of the twentieth century, such as jet plane travel, give an impression of rapid progress but until recent years such features were merely grafts on the island's senile body. Now, at the eleventh hour, a new treatment for the Corsican problem has been prescribed—integrated regional planning.

5   THE ECONOMY NOW AND TOMORROW

THE 'Corsican Problem' was defined in the previous chapter as chronic underdevelopment precipitated by the collapse of the traditional economy, the flight of population and the failure to exploit fully the island's resources. This problem reached a critical level by 1950. The population had dropped to a level comparable with that of the eighteenth century and not greatly larger than that of the sixteenth century. Since 1950, positive action, both planned and spontaneous, has been taken in attempts to reverse the downward spiral. This chapter attempts to summarise the pattern of economic activity which confronts the contemporary visitor and to gauge the success of the effort to revive the island's fortunes.

A traveller visiting the island, especially outside the main tourist season, might well demand how Corsica gains a livelihood. In the winter months it appears to be in a state of economic repose. The traffic in the ports and airports is reduced, most of the hotels are closed, and the countryside appears more than ever deserted. In fact, on the basis of its productive economic activity, Corsica does not pay her way.

THE ISLAND'S INCOME

Of the cash income accruing to Corsicans each year, only approximately 55 per cent is earned from employment in the island. The remainder of the income is made up by invisible items of which pensions are by far the most important. The balance of trade is in constant heavy deficit, for over half the food supplies and almost all consumer goods are imported, while only cheese, wines and timber are exported in significant quantity.

The total labour force in 1968 was only around 50,000 strong, rather more than a quarter of the whole population. The agricultural sector, including forestry, comprises the largest single group of workers, totalling approximately 16,000. However, with over 30 per cent of the island work force, it accounts for only 5 per cent of the total income. Here lies the legacy of the exodus for, setting aside the shepherds and the farmers on the reclaimed lowlands, the majority of those who are classed as agriculturalists eke out an existence on holdings that are too small and fragmented to be viable. Many are farmers in name rather than in reality and depend on their land for subsistence rather than for income.

The manpower employed in public services, about 10,000 workers, is the next largest work sector. It comprises civil servants, school teachers, employees in the health service and local government, and the military. As a group, these predominantly urban dwellers gain more than double the total income earned by agricultural activity. Commercial and business employment, other than tourism, employs over 7,000 people, who receive approximately 14 per cent of the island's annual income, while tourism and personal services employ approximately 4,000 workers and earn 10 per cent of the total island income. Tourism is clearly a remunerative activity, earning double the amount derived from agriculture with a labour force only a quarter the size of that sector. The building industry, including public works, employs nearly 7,000 workers which reflects the expansion of construction for the tourist industry and the large labour force recruited for building barrages, irrigation systems and new farms.

The earnings of the island's labour force account for little more than half Corsica's total earnings and the 'hole' in the economy is plugged by income unrelated to employment in the island. That pensions of various kinds account for the greater part of this additional income is due to the high average age of the population. Forty per cent of the people are over the age of forty-four,

85

and 23,000 inhabitants have passed the age of retirement on a state pension. The normal retirement pension, together with professional pensions, earned during careers in civil or military service, account for a substantial flow of money into the island. To these must be added a much smaller amount in remissions from relatives on the mainland, capital repatriated by Corsicans retiring from abroad, and profits from outside investment. Without this very substantial income, derived outside normal productive activity, the island could not support even its present size of population. The combination of earned income and pensions enabled Corsica to achieve an average income of £410 (US $1,120) per head of population in 1968, a by no means negligible figure. Unemployment is almost non-existent, although this must be attributed to the emigration of people of working age rather than to the strength of the economy. In fact economic conditions vary from one sector of activity to another, from a state of extreme frailty to one of real promise.

AGRICULTURE

Under 10 per cent of Corsica is now under cultivation, and even this estimate includes large areas of olive groves and orchards in various stages of decay. It is indeed doubtful whether the area devoted to productive arable use, including vineyards, orchards and market gardens, exceeds 5 per cent of the land area. Approximately 40 per cent of the island can be classified as pasture, but much of this is mountain grazing of low carrying capacity or rough grazing on abandoned fields that are in the process of degrading into maquis. Almost 20 per cent of the land is covered by virtually unproductive maquis and the forested area, accounting for almost 30 per cent of the total, includes only a small proportion of commercial plantation.

Pastoral farming

As far as the value of agricultural production is concerned, two types of enterprise, pastoralism and viticulture, have long been the backbone of the agricultural economy. Pastoralism is Corsica's most traditional form of agriculture with roots lost in antiquity. Ironically, it is the shepherd, using methods unchanged for centuries, who now enjoys the most viable agricultural enterprise. Since 1893, the *pâte* made from ewe's milk has been bought by the *Société des Caves et Producteurs réunis de Roquefort* which operates a network of dairies. Just under 2,000 tons of *pâte* are exported to mainland France each year for the manufacture of Roquefort cheese, guaranteeing the shepherds a steady cash income. With its extensive use of land, lower labour requirement, and orientation towards the export market, pastoralism has been better able to survive the exodus of population than has sedentary agriculture. There were approximately 150,000 sheep in the island in 1968, as compared with almost half a million at the turn of the century; the number of goats has also declined to the present total of 40,000. Nevertheless, the shepherd makes a good living and is the envy of other farmers.

In the past, the renting of fields lying fallow satisfied the shepherd's need of winter pasture and was at the same time a means of getting the soil manured. As arable farming has declined, many farmers have continued to rent their disused fields to the shepherds, thus achieving an income which requires no effort. On the plains where land reclamation is progressing, however, the shepherd is experiencing difficulty in renting land in his traditional winter pasturing areas and this has increasingly led to the resort of burning the maquis to provide pasture, with attendant risks of forest fires. Throughout history the shepherds have been a disruptive element and generally unesteemed by their fellow Corsicans. Their rude life, the damage caused to land and forest by their wandering herds, the quarrels over water and grazing rights, their alleged responsibility for destructive fires—combined with a tinge of envy for their economic security—have all been sources of friction. Equally deplored in official circles is their reluctance to invest part of their substantial earnings in ways which would enable them to modernise their techniques.

THE ECONOMY NOW AND TOMORROW

Viticulture

Viticulture represents the opposite extreme to pastoralism in that it demands large amounts of labour and has recently been the object of modernisations intended to improve and standardise the quality of wine. The success of viticulture is owed to the ideal climate and the characteristic rich bouquet and high alcohol content of Corsican wine. The vineyards are of two kinds. In Cap Corse, the Nebbio, Sartenais and the district around Ajaccio, the traditional vineyards have long been established on terraced slopes. The emphasis in the industry there is now on more careful fermenting in order to produce a higher-quality wine, in the best instances with an *appellation contrôlée*. In contrast, on the new farms of the Casinca and Aleria plains, viticulture is practised on a plantation scale reminiscent of Languedoc. Emphasis here is on bulk production of ordinary wine, suited by its strength for blending. The average annual output of wine for the whole island is 700,000 hectolitres, of which 200,000hl are consumed directly on the farms, the remainder being marketed in the island or exported.

Orchards and market gardening

Two other types of farming are of commercial significance, orchards and market gardening. Tree farming has a long history, especially in the case of olives and cedrats. The cedrat plantations have almost completely disappeared and the output of the olive groves has been decimated through neglect and disease. The main area of modern olive production is the Ostriconi valley in the Balagne. On the other hand, the production of citrus and stone fruit has gained new impetus from the introduction of irrigated farming on the reclaimed eastern coastal plain. Apricots, peaches and oranges are grown there, and a considerable area is devoted to clementines. Market gardening is a feature of irrigated lowlands south of Ajaccio, in the Nebbio and on the Casinca and Marana plains. The growing of fresh vegetables and flowers can give a good return even on quite small holdings, and cut flowers are exported by air to mainland Europe.

Page 89 Death of a landscape: a mausoleum set among abandoned fields, Cap Corse

Page 90 Birth of a landscape: new farms, orchards and fields on the eastern plain

The survival of peasant farming

All the agricultural activities described so far are profitable and, with the exception of pastoralism, are adopting modern methods of production and co-operative marketing. The majority of the population officially recorded as 'agricultural proprietors' are however involved in an entirely different category of enterprise. These farmers are the survivors of the traditional self-sufficient peasant economy of the foothills, the chestnut zone and the interior valleys which, denuded of its labour force by migration and impoverished by the collapse of the local market for staple foods (especially cereals), survives in archaic form. Their holdings are small and much fragmented through subdivision at inheritance. Often the tree cover, usually the most valuable asset, was inherited by the eldest son, while the land on which it stood passed to other relations. The larger part of most holdings now lies unused under the encroaching maquis. Only terraced plots most accessible from the village are cultivated with vegetables, and with some corn for poultry feed, a few patches of vines provide wine for domestic use, and a few cattle, goats and pigs are grazed on a little mediocre pasture. This system of 'polyculture' is sufficient to provide a modest food supply with a minimum of effort and to yield a haphazard cash income from the sale of eggs, poultry, kid and cattle.

The traditional farmers are generally elderly and have little or no family or hired help; they are intensely conservative and generally cynical about land reform and technical improvement which would yield little benefit during their lifetime. There is frequently no prospect of an inheritor willing to take over the running of the holding. It is the inefficiency of such backward farming which accounts for the island's deficiencies in home-produced food, especially of dairy produce, veal and beef. Even much of the justly famed charcuterie is manufactured from imported pork. It is difficult to see much future for this decadent farming system, for it occupies the hill slopes, where irrigation is not feasible and mechanisation difficult. Its survival is only possible because of the supporting income of pensions and re-

F

91

missions from relatives, and it persists as a way of life rather than as a commercial enterprise.

As the older generation dies off, so the relics of traditional farming will disappear and the future of entire villages will be threatened. The regions where such conditions are most characteristic include wide areas of Cap Corse, interior Balagne, the Castagniccia and the middle Golo and Tavignano valleys. On the lower slopes and in the valleys where irrigation and land consolidation might be practicable, some improvement might be achieved, but on the upland and in the isolated valleys it is difficult to predict anything but further triumph for the advancing maquis.

Corsican agriculture is in the process of searching for a new equilibrium. The archaic polyculture of the interior seems bound to disappear for it is already in ruins. By contrast, new forms of farming, using irrigation and mechanised equipment, are being introduced on the coastal plains. They demand a new kind of operator, who must be a capitalist, businessman, technician and willing co-operator all in one, able to look to distant rather than to local markets. Such new farmers have no island tradition to fall back on; therefore there is a need not only for heavy investment in barrages, irrigation systems and machinery, but also for education to transform the techniques and psychology of the next generation of farmers.

FORESTRY

From the approaches to the island, especially by air, Corsica gives the appearance of being one vast forest, but this is an illusion for the verdant aspect owes as much to the commercially insignificant maquis as to the existence of forests. There are forests, it is true, and some are magnificent, but their value is greater as a scenic attraction than as an economic resource. The existing woodland, covering just under a third of the island, is the remnant of a once complete forest cover, much reduced by the depredations of both nature and man. Natural damage caused by avalanches and fire started by lightning have been less destructive than man's activities. The effects of centuries-long cutting for timber and charcoal burning have been exacerbated by the custom of grazing livestock in the forests which checks natural regrowth. Deliberate burning by shepherds has destroyed thousands of hectares of woodland which are now covered by scrub.

The most extensive remaining forests are those of Aitone, Vizzavona, Ghisoni, Valdo Niello, Bavella and Zonza. Corsican pine and cork oak, the latter found in plantations near Porto-Vecchio, are the most important woods now exploited. The forestry industry is frustrated by the slow rate of new plantation, owing to problems of access, cost and shortage of tree nurseries. Above all the protection of the forests against inroads by livestock and the perennial problem of fire appear to be almost insuperable problems. The value of forest production is lower than that of livestock products and, for lack of effective control, forestry and the pastoral industry are perpetually in mutual conflict.

FISHING

Fishing is only a minor activity and of the total fleet of 300 boats, almost all are of less than ten tons. There are approximately ten in-shore trawlers, landing tunny and sardines, but the majority of the small vessels catch rock fish and *langouste*. Ajaccio has by far the largest fleet, followed by Bastia, Bonifacio, Propriano, Cargese and Calvi. The industry is hampered by limited facilities for refrigeration, without which internal distribution and export are both difficult. The *étangs* of Biguglia and Diane are exploited for their eels, while river and undersea fishing are tourist occupations rather than commercial enterprises.

MANUFACTURING

Industry employs only 4,000 persons and most visitors leave the island without having seen a factory. The reasons are not hard

93

to find. There are few industrial resources, and many of those that do exist are scarcely exploited. Deposits of amianthus, a fine variety of asbestos, occur on the western coast of Cap Corse. The extraction of this mineral at a mine at Canari employed over 300 workers. It was exported through Bastia, but the import into France of cheaper Canadian supplies forced the closure of the mine in 1965. The island also possesses several good mineral springs which are used for a rather desultory spa activity, but only at Orezza, in the Castagniccia, is mineral water now bottled for distribution.

Lacking a genuine industrial tradition, the old craft industries are largely extinguished. Away from Bastia, industry is limited very largely to small timber mills and production of building materials. In the suburbs of Bastia there are modern factories, although small in scale. They include the Job cigarette factory which processes all the island's tobacco crop, producing 45 million packets a year, and the Mattei factory, bottling wine and manufacturing liqueurs and apéritifs. A sign, perhaps, of a more promising future for industry is the new fruit and vegetable pre-serving factory at Casamozza, on the banks of the Golo near Bastia airport. This co-operative venture was built to process the produce of the new farms of the coastal plain and is one of the most modern plants in Europe.

TOURISM

Official guides and the brochures issued by tour operators com-pete in extolling Corsica as a tourist's paradise. Their exaggera-tions are in fact slight for Corsica does offer most things that the average tourist could legitimately expect. Not surprisingly tourism is officially regarded as a 'lever' for the island's economy, both for the financial returns it brings and for the impetus it gives to the construction industry, transport and the whole range of per-sonal and trading services. It is estimated that in 1968 tourism earned 125 million francs for the economy and that a total of over eight million tourist-days were spent in the island. When it is considered that in 1939 a mere 48,000 visitors were recorded, this is no mean achievement in a fiercely competitive international industry. The island's natural vocation for tourism is beyond dispute. Constantly fine weather is virtually assured throughout the summer months and the potential tourist season runs from April until the end of September. About a third of the 1,000 kilometres of coastline consists of good sandy beaches and these are backed by impressive mountain scenery which gives a landscape setting that will stand comparison with any other tourist region of Europe. Throughout the decade 1950–60, after the post-war difficulties of foreign travel had been removed, tourism was still dependant on a limited number of hotels in the main towns, many of which were by no means the last word in modernity. Much of the rapid expansion in tourism during that decade was based on *camping sauvage*, which created no employment and brought little revenue to the island. After 1960 however, there was a boom in construction. This has created much-needed extra tourist accommodation and introduced new forms of holidaymaking. By 1970 the number of classified hotels approached 200 and over a hundred unclassified hotels swelled the total number of rooms to approximately 7,000. There were over forty official camp sites with space for 13,500 campers and fifteen holiday hostels for young children.

The greatest innovations were the chalet complexes and holiday villages. The chalet complexes vary in style and quality from groups of rudimentary bungalows with communal amenities to well-equipped villas built not only for renting but also for purchase as holiday homes. Between these extremes, the holiday villages, of the type pioneered by the *Club Méditerrannée*, lay emphasis on organised recreation, including marine sports, and an animated informal night life. The holiday village 'formula' has been developed particularly in association with inclusive tour operation.

This latest wave of tourism began in the established centres, with Calvi as the prototype. There a chain of holiday villages

and camps lines the coastal *pinède* to the east of the ancient citadelle and development on a smaller scale has occurred at Algajola and l'Ile-Rousse. Between these centres, many new private
villas grace the *marines* of the Balagne coast. A similar pattern
borders the Gulf of Ajaccio, from the Iles Sanguinaires to Pointe
della Castagna. In the latest developments, however, both new
hotels and holiday villages have been built in coastal areas previously untouched by tourism, and in some instances on entirely
virgin stretches of coast. Examples are Propriano, Porto-Vecchio
and the lagoon of Biguglia. By 1970, the holiday villages and
chalet complexes provided almost 5,000 rooms.

Impressive though many of the new developments are this is
not to say that the tourist industry does not face problems. The
total capacity of accommodation at any given time in the season
may be generously estimated at some 24,000 places, of which
over half are in camping sites. This is by no means adequate for
the potential number of tourists, and it is already clear that a
substantial number of people visiting the island do so outside the
organised holiday industry. Chief of these are Corsicans, returning
annually to visit relatives, and campers who do not use organised
sites. It is probable that as many as 30 per cent of the visitors do
not participate in the hotel and allied commercial activity, and
do not make a high contribution to the economy.

Another serious problem is the discrepancy in tourist activity
between the coast and the interior. Most tourists are, of course,
attracted to the island in search of sun and sea and their visits
to the interior tend to be limited to excursions along celebrated
itineraries with at most one or two overnight stops. There are
large areas which may be termed 'non-tourist', not because they
lack features of attraction but because they are ill equipped in
terms of accommodation and serviceable roads. Yet so much of
Corsica's history and folk-lore belongs to the interior, so much
magnificent scenery is to be found there, that to hug the coast is
to turn one's back on the authentic Corsica in favour of a synthetic and cosmopolitan intrusion where only the sun is geniunely
Corsican. Efforts are now being made to promote tourism in the

interior, as for example in the development of winter sports at Asco and alpinism at the Col de Vergio, but the number of tourists attracted there is but a fraction of those who flock to the coast. The latest attempt to popularise the interior is the creation of a regional park, sweeping diagonally across the island from the forest of Ospedale in the south-east to the Fango valley in the north-west, encompassing some 1,520 square kilometres (375,000 acres). The park has a multiple purpose, involving conservation, the creation of employment in areas of depopulation, and the promotion of an entirely rural form of tourism based on wildlife study, climbing, naturism, hunting and fishing. The most difficult problem is likely to be that of convincing the Corsicans themselves, particularly the shepherds, of the viability and utility of the park and thus making it compatible with the traditional pastoral economy. Ironically, the success of the park depends more on educating the indigenous population to respect their threatened environment, and on curbing their proclivity to destroy its resources by burning and overgrazing, than on controlling use of the park by visitors.

An apparent lack of enthusiasm on the part of the Corsicans themselves inhibits the growth of tourism. In part this reflects a lack of experience, especially among rural people, of management, the art of cuisine and the organisation of personal services generally. It is symptomatic of this background that the island's foremost hotel, the Napoléon Bonaparte at l'Ile-Rousse, closed down in 1966, to be reopened in 1968 as an hotel school. The problem is not merely one of aptitude, but also of temperament. Corsicans are extremely hospitable by nature, but when it comes to employment a position of command, however limited in scope, is always preferred to the more humble position of giving service at the command of others—hence the continued preference for careers in the civil service, with its less onerous work, greater status and the all-important pension.

Tourism remains the great promise for the future but thus far a frustration to the economic planners. Expansion has been handicapped by shortage of capital, transport difficulties and by a less than wholehearted response from Corsicans to this new opportunity. Growth during 1960–70 created fewer than 5,000 new jobs, located overwhelmingly at the coast. When compared with the 100 kilometres or so of coastline at the Riviera or Costa Brava, the development of Corsica's 1,000 kilometres of coast and undeveloped interior seems embryonic indeed. The island has been fortunate in being able to accommodate its tourist developments without overcrowding or obtrusiveness, partly because there was little pre-war tourist development and the density of resident population is so low, partly because the developments have been very dispersed geographically. The physical overcrowding of beaches and roads has not been one of the island's problems, an advantage Corsica has had over the Riviera. The fact that tourism has not mushroomed overnight has very largely spared the island from tawdry unplanned construction. As yet Corsica remains unspoilt and the beauty of the environment has not been compromised.

PLANNED DEVELOPMENT SINCE 1957

Planning is by no means new to Corsica. Many plans have flitted across the island scene since its attachment to France, and even earlier, under the aegis of the Genoese and of Paoli. What has been lacking has been action based on the plans. The mass emigration of Corsicans is in part to be attributed to the neglect of past governments; they have been ready to study and document the 'Corsican Problem' but lacked concern for its solution. Against this background of a people who have practically lost faith in official plans, it is possible to view the present planning endeavour with both admiration and cynicism. One can readily admire individual achievments, whether luxury hotels or pioneer farms, but one is tempted to be cynical about the discrepancy in scale between these achievements and the magnitude of the problem of underdevelopment

Official regional planning dates from 1957. In this year a plan was published, defining two major lines of action. The expansion of tourism was seen as a means of rapid economic growth, of attracting capital and population and of swelling the internal market for food supplies and a wide range of services. Alongside this expansion the reclamation of coastal lowlands for intensive agriculture was seen as a means of increasing food supplies, and in the long term yielding a substantial surplus for export. The original feature of this plan, compared with previous ill-fated attempts, was that, recognising the deficiencies of the island's financial, administrative and technical resources, two development companies were created, responsible respectively for tourist development and agricultural rehabilitation.

Tourist development

The ambitious target set in 1957 for the tourist development corporation was the creation of a hundred new hotels with 3,000 rooms in the space of five years. Work has been consistently hampered by inadequate government funds, and by 1970 the target of a total of 5,000 hotel rooms in the island had not been met. The corporation has built some half dozen luxury hotels and has aided the financing and construction of other hotels, holiday villages and tourist complexes. In spite of the unfulfilled target, the corporation must be credited with promoting a standard of accommodation hitherto unknown in the island. It has also pioneered new kinds of amenities, such as yacht marinas, game reserves and winter sports facilities.

Land reclamation and colonisation

The renovation of agriculture could scarcely be achieved overnight, for the task of the development corporation was to put into production areas of the eastern coastal plain abandoned for centuries and, until 1945, the scene of endemic malaria. This scheme required elaborate research into climatic and drainage conditions, a complete study of the soils and experimental work on the selection of appropriate crops. Alternating between ill-drained swamp in winter and semi-aridity in summer, the plain required both drainage and irrigation works. In the twelve years after work

99

started in 1957, the achievements were quite startling in an island accustomed more to the abandonment of land than to its reclamation. On the plain of Aleria huge perimeters were carved out of the maquis at Ghisonaccia and Linguizetta and over a hundred new farms were built. More than a hundred run-down farms on the plain have been rebuilt and equipped for irrigation. Altogether over 6,000ha (15,000 acres) of previously useless land were converted to irrigated agriculture, producing citrus fruit, vines, soft fruit, vegetables and flowers.

The process of reclamation and colonisation has produced some unexpected problems. It might have been expected that the Corsicans would have responded enthusiastically to the possibility of operating modern farms. In fact this was not the case initially, for the local farming community viewed with cynicism the attempt to cultivate a region traditionally regarded as valueless. It was also difficult to find prospective farmers with sufficient capital or credit to afford the payments for the farms, especially in the first years before the tree crops could come into production. This lack on the one hand of faith and imagination and on the other of hard cash threatened to compromise the scheme.

By good fortune, the initial phase of the scheme coincided with the return of French repatriates from Algeria in the early 1960s. As an act of solidarity, these *pieds noirs* received generous resettlement grants and low interest loans, which enabled many repatriates to seize the opportunity to re-establish themselves. Being already skilled in irrigated farming and versed in commercial production, the *pieds noirs* achieved yields that soon confounded the doubts formerly expressed by Corsican farmers. The success of the *pieds noirs* was viewed with a rather jaundiced eye, and the original scepticism has given way to the complaint that the island's wealth is passing into the hands of outsiders.

Of the first hundred new farms occupied, roughly three-quarters were allocated to Algerian repatriates, mainly of Corsican origin. Considerable agitation and some violence has marked this dispute between the development corporation and dissatisfied

Corsicans, frustrated by their inability to obtain low interest loans equivalent to those disbursed to the *pieds noirs*. The undoubted success of the reclamation project, which has boosted wine and citrus fruit production substantially, has thus been achieved at the expense of yet further disenchantment of Corsicans *vis-à-vis* the government administration.

THE FUTURE—NEO-COLONIALISM OR REGIONALISM

The two main elements of the island's plan, the expansion of tourism and the reclamation of land for agriculture, are being achieved, even if lack of government funds has caused the time-table to slip. Yet there is little sign that the life of the average Corsican has been affected for the better by more than a decade of economic planning. On the contrary, the criticisms and complaints directed at the government and its agencies on the island have grown steadily more militant. In the first half of 1970 over a dozen explosions and fires disturbed the island's peace; they were claimed to be the work of a 'Liberation Committee'. These outrages have not been indiscriminate but were directed against certain symbols of the alleged problems of the island. The head-quarters of the agricultural development corporation at Bastia and a model sheep farm owned by a *pied noir* were both set alight in 1970. The *sous-préfecture* at Bastia has also been subjected to bomb attack as a gesture against the alleged ineptitude of the island administration, as well as an hotel owned by the Compagnie Générale Transatlantique which enjoys a monopoly of passenger shipping services to the mainland. It remains to be seen whether these outbursts are merely manifestations of the latent violence inherited from the past or have serious new political implications.

There are no mass movements for autonomy but there is a growing 'regionalist' movement. This latter has as its basis a cata-logue of complaints, ranging from weak government, the corrup-tion of politics dominated by clan loyalties, the inadequacies of

101

the road system, and the lack of higher education facilities, to the yearning for a 'regional' status akin to that of Sardinia, which enjoys large government subventions and a degree of autonomy in their application. Underlying the agitation is the fear that Corsica is reverting to the position of a colony as opposed to an integral *département* of metropolitan France.

To many Corsicans the island's economic plans seem to be unrelated to the aspirations and capacities of the indigenous population and their processes seem to be undemocratic. The chosen sectors for development—tourism and intensive agriculture—are highly competitive activities which also require substantial initial investment. Participation by Corsicans therefore presupposes commercial experience and access to capital; attributes lacking in the majority of cases. Not surprisingly, many of the achievements of planning have been attained through the application of skills, capital and management from outside the island, and the benefits have in consequence accrued to outsiders. The actual plans are conceived by technocrats and appear to be administered only in the interests of outsiders, whether *pieds noirs* or big business. Meanwhile the indigenous population must endure the defective road system, the enforced exodus for work and higher education, and the steady erosion of Corsican culture. This view, however exaggerated, is readily dramatised and gives a platform to the regionalist groups with their slogans of *Corsica Nostra*.

Yet it is difficult to see what other course was open to the planners of the island's future but to accept capital and settlers from outside. In attempting to modernise the economy, the plans uncovered a lacuna, a lack of expertise and capital, which could be filled only from outside. At the end of the day, rhetoric and noble sentiments are less efficacious than skills, investment and the will to succeed. Planned economic growth therefore might leave a legacy of an ideological battle between the administrators and technocrats, who see in outside investment a healthy trend towards new ideas and energies, and sections of the indigenous population, who regard this same process as but a new phase of exploitation. According to one's standpoint in this argument, it is possible to portray Corsica as an embryonic California, with its new vineyards, citrus groves and luxury beach hotels, or as another French Algeria, with its deserted interior lands and its wealth concentrated in the hands of a relatively few *colons* and business corporations.

6 THE TOWNS AND URBAN LIFE

MEDITERRANEAN civilisation is intimately linked with an urban culture extending back into antiquity. In this respect, however, Corsica is an exception, for the island lacks a strong indigenous urban tradition. Although the majority of Corsicans now live in towns, this is a relatively modern feature, reflecting a generation of rural depopulation rather than a strong attachment throughout history to urban life. Almost all Corsican towns were founded by occupying powers rather than spontaneous outgrowths of the internal economy and culture. Of the principal towns, only Corte and Sartène may be considered as having evolved out of the traditional pattern of life. The reasons underlying this apparent lack of an impetus towards urbanisation on the part of Corsicans are not difficult to find.

The natural physique of the island fragments the landscape into small units. Throughout history these physical compartments isolated population groups one from another, inhibiting the social and economic intercourse that is the basis of urban organisation; and the administrative structure of the *pièves*, consisting of groups of villages and hamlets which were largely self-sufficient in the material needs of life, reduced the need to have towns as centres of commerce and exchange until late in the island's history. The exploitation of the sea figured only slightly in the indigenous land-based Corsican economy, and hence the growth of ports as a springboard for urban development was only weakly developed. Rather did the coastline, with its alternation of rocky promontories and malarial swamp, inject an element of insecurity into the island's life, in terms both of health hazard and vulnerability to outside attack.

The earliest urban settlements were those founded on the shores of the eastern plain by the Greeks and Romans, as has been recounted in an earlier chapter. The outlines of Aleria and Mariana have been revealed by recent excavations to have consisted in both cases of two elements—a residential area several kilometres inland and a port on the coast where a lagoon offered sheltered anchorages. Aleria may have housed as many as 20,000 inhabitants. Until further research reveals more evidence, a certain amount of ambiguity surrounds the scale of urban development during the Roman period, but it is established that Aleria and Mariana were the principal centres of colonisation and the key elements in control of the island. With the decline of Roman power, a period of renewed barbarian invasion ensued during which urban civilisation was virtually extinguished and remained so until the arrival of Genoese colonisers in the thirteenth century.

GENOESE STRONGHOLDS

Interested primarily in obtaining secure bases, the Genoese ignored past urban sites in favour of readily fortified positions, even where the hinterland was comparatively unproductive. The first two foundations, Bonifacio (1195) and Calvi (1268), were built at opposite ends of the island, both invaluable as strategic locations for controlling sea routes but possessing strictly limited hinterlands. Later foundations at Bastia (1380), St Florent (1440), Ajaccio (1492) and Porto-Vecchio (1539), completed a chain of coastal towns, inspired more by a preoccupation with strategic maritime interests than with the internal exploitation of the island's resources. These towns were essentially fortresses commanding ports or anchorages; they were all dominated by massive citadelles which remain to this day the most distinctive feature of Corsica's urban landscape.

In search of natural security the Genoese built their fortresses characteristically on promontories, protected on three sides by the sea. This feature is best exemplified at Bonifacio, where unscalable cliffs add to the impregnability of the peninsular site, and at Calvi, where the citadelle surmounts a rocky headland. The function of the citadelle was at first the protection of the adjacent harbour, but in due course the fortifications enclosed urban communities. The interior structure of the citadelle tends to follow an orderly grid pattern of streets in which the focal points tend to be a cathedral or a large church, and an open square, commonly adjacent to the main defensive bastion. In some cases, as at Bastia and Calvi, the citadelle enclosed the whole of the old cité within its ramparts. In others, as at Ajaccio and Bonifacio, the heavily fortified citadelle can be distinguished from the adjacent *hauteville*, which shared the same defensive site but lacked massive artificial fortifications.

THE CORSICANS BUILD TOWNS

The Genoese occupation was in large measure responsible for a further stage in the development of town building by the Corsicans themselves. Prior to the Genoese conquest, the basic settlement pattern consisted of villages and hamlets inhabited by shepherds and cultivators. By virtue of their strategic location in relation to the convergence of valley routes or important mountain passes, some villages gained an importance that extended beyond their immediate confines. A few of them, such as Vescovato in the northern Castagniccia, were bishoprics, but whatever factor enhanced their standing, these larger villages remained throughout the Middle Ages essentially agricultural in function and modest in size. The period of upheaval which accompanied the Genoese occupation of the interior, and the renewed struggles for independence as Genoese dominance began to wane, were propitious for urban development in a society which hitherto had felt little need for towns. The conflict between feudal lords and Genoese power gave rise to centres of Corsican opposition and resistance which in some instances assumed certain urban characteristics.

The supreme example of these is Corte, the very heart of the island both geographically and in terms of the indigenous Corsican

106

Page 107 A narrow street in the citadelle, Bastia

Page 108 Aerial view of the Bastia agglomeration

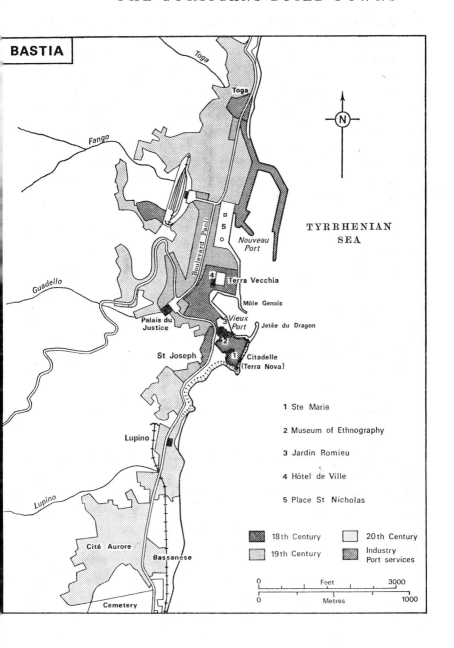

BASTIA

Toga

Toga

Fango

Guadello

Boulevard Paoli

5

Nouveau
Port

TYRRHENIAN
SEA

N

4 Terra Vecchia

Môle Genois

Palais du
Justice

Vieux
Port

Jetée du Dragon

3

St Joseph

2

1 Citadelle
(Terra Nova)

Lupino

Lupino

Cité Aurore

Bassanese

Cemetery

1 Ste Marie

2 Museum of Ethnography

3 Jardin Romieu

4 Hôtel de Ville

5 Place St Nicholas

18th Century

19th Century

20th Century

Industry
Port services

0	Feet	3000
0	Metres	1000

G

culture. It is doubtful whether any other site in the island could have been more destined by natural features to become the location of a town. The town is situated on the summit and flank of a massive crag near the confluences of the Tavignano, Restonica and Orta rivers. It is protected by water on three sides while the citadelle surmounts an impregnable crag surveying a vast panorama of the surrounding valleys. The town's situation at the focus of natural routeways also stamps Corte as the virtual crossroads of the island, for it commands the central furrow aligned north and south at the point where it intersects with the only practicable east-west route from Bastia to Ajaccio. To the north-east the Golo valley gives access to Bastia, and north-westwards, via the Col de St Columbano, to the Balagne and Calvi. To the south-west, the Col de Vizzavona gives on to the Gravone valley and Ajaccio. To the south-east, the Tavignano valley skirts the Castagniccia to reach the Plain of Aleria.

In spite of these obvious advantages of both site and situation, it required the stimulus of resistance to outside dominance to transform Corte from an agricultural and pastoral village into a town and capital of the interior. The citadelle was built in 1420 by Vincentello d'Istria, an Aragonese viceroy, sheltering the old town to the south and east. In the next 300 years the town suffered capture by the Genoese on two occasions and in 1734 it was taken by the French army. Retaken by the Corsicans in 1745, Corte became the capital of the short-lived independent nation from 1755 to 1769, when Paoli established the island government and founded a university there. By the end of the eighteenth century the town had a population of approximately 2,000 inhabitants.

Although much less impressive in terms of its site and historical role, Sartène also rose to the status of a town by virtue of its involvement in the struggle between the local feudal patriarchs and outside attack. Sartène lacks the natural defensive features of Corte, having been built on a slope overlooking the Rizzanese valley and the Gulf of Valinco. The early history of Sartène was punctuated by barbarian attack from the sea, and the town was fortified in the sixteenth century. Situated on an important route between the uplands and coastal lowlands, the migrant shepherds on their seasonal passage with the flocks used the town as a stage for the exchange of produce. While direct conflict with the Genoese was avoided, Sartène represented a consolidation, for the sake of security, of traditional land-owning patriarchal groups who had been conditioned throughout history to external threats. By the end of the eighteenth century the town had 1,200 inhabitants, overwhelmingly concerned with agriculture.

Whereas both Corte and Sartène developed in response to resistance to external threats, the third native Corsican town, l'Ile-Rousse, was a deliberate political foundation. Following his policy of isolating the free Corsican nation from the Genoese strongholds in the coastal towns, Paoli conceived l'Ile-Rousse in 1758 as a Corsican rival to Calvi. The new town was situated on the northern coast of the fertile Balagne region. A group of small islands provided a sheltered port, to the south of which the town was laid out to a rectilinear pattern. As a defensive site, l'Ile-Rousse was markedly inferior to Calvi, but its hinterland was more productive and at first the port prospered at the expense of its rival. People were attracted to it from the villages of the Balagne and Cap Corse and, had Paoli's financial resources been more substantial and his independent republic more durable, the town might well have grown impressively. Instead, the republic proved ephemeral, Corte was relegated from being capital of the island and, under the French, the impetus derived from Paoli was dissipated. L'Ile-Rousse never attained its intended status once the political motivation was removed.

By the close of the eighteenth century, Corsica had achieved the present outline of urban centres and no new towns have been added since. Out of an island population of approximately 150,000 in 1785, the seven largest towns housed only 23,000 inhabitants. With over 8,000 inhabitants, Bastia was almost twice as populous as the second largest town, Ajaccio. Bonifacio had 3,000 inhabitants but all the remaining centres had fewer than 2,000 inhabitants each. In spite of their crucial role during and immediately after the Genoese occupation, the growth of towns in Corsica left untouched the vast majority of the population. Throughout almost all the nineteenth century population steadily expanded: from 165,000 in 1800, it reached 280,000 by 1880. The extent to which the towns participated in this expansion varied considerably. While the population of Bastia tripled during the century to 25,000, and that of Ajaccio grew five-fold to 22,000, the smaller towns remained relatively stagnant. Corte and Sartène attained 5,000 inhabitants but Bonifacio and Calvi remained almost stationary. Under Napoleon's patronage as the island capital, Ajaccio made headway against Bastia but never succeeded in overtaking the latter as the island's largest town. The nineteenth century was notable for the spilling out of towns beyond their fortifications and in some cases the *extramuros* sections exceeded in area and population those of the citadelles. During the century the towns also ceased to house a large agricultural population as employment in transport, commerce and small-scale industries developed. Even the smaller towns of Corte and Sartène lost their rural aspect and the daily exodus of farmers descending to the surrounding fields became less apparent. The expansion of the urban built-up areas was thus accompanied by a profound change in the social structure of the towns.

TWENTIETH-CENTURY URBAN GROWTH

The year 1880 marked a watershed in the island's demographic history as being the approximate date of maximum population after which a prolonged decline was experienced. As has already been shown, this decline was an exclusively rural phenomenon, the towns continuing to grow. Whereas the initial founding of towns stemmed from strategic considerations and their subsequent growth was as centres for surrounding agricultural areas, urban expansion during the present century has been specifically related to fundamental changes in the island's economy. The decay of agriculture provoked a rural exodus which nourished the towns with migrants. This decline of villages and the growth of towns represented a redistribution of population from a depressed farming economy to the growing employment opportunities of the coastal towns. There is nothing unique in such a rural-urban redistribution, which is a universal trend within twentieth-century Europe, but two features of this process in Corsica make it remarkable. Firstly, the scale of redistribution was very large; from being little more than 15 per cent urban in 1900, a proportion constant since 1785, over 55 per cent of the population now resides in towns. Secondly the normal stimulus to rural-urban migration—industrial development in the towns—has been almost entirely lacking in Corsica. For example, in Bastia, the most industrialised town in the island, less than 10 per cent of the labour force is employed in manufacturing. Rural-urban migration must be seen as an exodus from the countryside, and it was natural that the main towns and ports, especially Bastia and Ajaccio, should intercept some of the stream of migrants, the majority of whom were headed for destinations on the mainland.

The run-down of the island's agriculture led to an increasing reliance on imported foodstuffs as the urban population grew, while the failure of modern industry to develop necessitated the import of consumer goods and machinery. The result was to stimulate the transport industry, and particularly employment connected with the ports. The import trade created employment not only in cargo handling, but also in more qualified activities such as shipping agencies, insurance and wholesaling. The need for the distribution of imported goods stimulated employment in land transport, especially in the two major port towns, Bastia and Ajaccio.

Further growth in these two ports has also resulted from their enlarged functions as administrative centres for both public and private sectors. Both Ajaccio, the island capital, and Bastia, the most important *sous-préfecture*, employ large numbers of workers who may be termed civil servants. In the private sector, these towns contain the head offices of all the important businesses.

113

Besides this the fact that Bastia and Ajaccio have throughout the last century been so much larger than any of the other towns has resulted in their being chosen as the centres for important services, such as hospitals and colleges to serve very large tributary areas, further swelling the importance of professional and service employment in the two ports.

Important though transport and administration have been as factors promoting the ability of Bastia and Ajaccio to absorb population increase, the largest single growth has been in the general category of commerce. The range of retailing establishments is particularly remarkable, from air-conditioned department stores to dingy street corner shops, and from luxury restaurants to tiny bars which consist of little more than one table placed on the pavement. The character of retailing is undergoing profound changes. Refrigerated ships now permit the importing of perishable goods in bulk, supplying a growing number of supermarkets. Increased sales of consumer goods has stimulated the expansion of large department stores, with sufficient capital to carry large stocks—an impossibility for the smaller businesses. The past proliferation of small businesses, lining virtually every back street and absorbing large amounts of family labour, now has to compete with the growth of larger enterprises employing paid labour.

Indeed, many of the smaller businesses, which have contributed so much to employment growth in the past, now appear to have a tenuous hold on life and many seem bound soon to disappear. Their survival thus far may be attributed to several factors, of which the persistence of neighbourhood ties, especially in the case of food shops and bars, is one of the most important. Also, in the case of many small enterprises, the running of a business is combined with other sources of income—a fishing boat, the letting of rooms or, of course, a pension.

From the foregoing it is clear that urban expansion in the present century has been related largely to increased employment in service activities rather than to industrial developments, the continuously though gradually increasing town populations demanding the provision of more and more services and perpetually creating more jobs. The towns have not all experienced the stimulus to growth in equal force; the special cases of Ajaccio and Bastia, with their particular administrative functions, have already been noted. The differences in local commercial and tourist development have in some measure given the towns their present-day distinctive character.

BASTIA

Situated at the south-eastern base of the Cap Corse peninsula and hemmed in between steep mountains and the sea, Bastia has grown far beyond its original nucleus beside a small natural inlet. The town now extends north-south along a narrow coastal plain for a distance of four kilometres. In atmosphere and functions, Bastia contrasts sharply with Ajaccio. As the administrative capital and focus of the tourist industry, Ajaccio has an almost bourgeois atmosphere; Bastia, the commercial centre of the island, has rather less charm and a more specifically working-class population. The first settlement was a small fishing village, situated at the mouth of the Guadello stream, which now constitutes the Vieux Port. This settlement, the Marine de Cardo, was a dependent of the hillside village of Cardo, some five kilometres inland. From this modest beginning, the Genoese transformed the settlement into a military and commercial port, the administrative capital and largest town of the island.

Besides being an excellent strategic location from which to control the Ligurian and Tyrrhenian seas, the Guadello creek offered one of the few natural harbours, however imperfect, between the rocky coastline of Cap Corse to the north, and the inhospitable plain to the south. The name Bastia derives from *bastiglia* (a dungeon), recalling that at the outset, the settlement was a fortress rather than a town. The site chosen by the Genoese was the promontory flanking the southern shore of the Guadello, offering at once a defensive position, surrounded on three sides by water, and a standpoint from which to command the entrance

115

to the harbour. Here in 1380 was built the dungeon, protecting the Governor's Palace. As the community in the lee of the bastion grew, so the fortifications were extended until in 1521 the town was completely encompassed by the walls and the outline of the citadelle was established. The title Terra Nova was bestowed on the fortified town, distinguishing it from the external *quartiers* which developed outside the walls and in particular around the Vieux Port. The restrictions of the citadelle site imposed a high density of building, with narrow streets and few open spaces. The only large public open space today is at the entrance to the citadelle in the shadow of the dungeon, the present-day Place du Donjon.

The initial growth of the town outside the citadelle was largely a result of the limited amount of space contained within the walls, legal restrictions limiting Corsican residence within Terra Nova, and also the undesirability of accommodating certain types of land use, such as the cemetery, abattoirs and gibbet, inside the fortified town. External growth resulted more particularly from the development of the port and the establishment of numerous convents and monasteries. Under Genoese rule, Bastia grew around the Vieux Port, the new streets following the contours in semi-circular fashion, and to the north of the port in the *quartier* of Terra Vecchia. The defence of these external, unfortified *quartiers* was assured by a chain of four hilltop forts that overlooked the entire town. By the middle of the eighteenth century, the *extra-muros* parts of the town greatly exceeded the walled citadelle in area and the total population of the entire settlement had attained 7,000.

The combined functions of garrison town, commercial port and administrative capital, together with its increasing importance as a regional centre for a productive agricultural hinterland, ensured the supremacy of Bastia during the later part of the Genoese occupation. After the achievement of independence and incorporation into France, a marked cadence ensued in the rate of growth. In 1811, Bastia lost its status of island capital to Ajaccio and was reduced to the rank of *sous-préfecture*. The first

116

half of the nineteenth century was thus a period of slow progress during which Ajaccio expanded more rapidly in terms of population, public building and transport facilities.

By contrast, the second half of the century witnessed renewed growth during which many of the present features of Bastia appeared. A new road was engineered to the west of Terra Vecchia, giving improved access to the town, and providing a new north-south axis, the present-day Boulevard Paoli, across the Plain of St Nicolas. During this time, the silting up of the Vieux Port, coinciding with the need to improve port facilities to support a new foundry at Toga to the north of Bastia, led to the commencement of work on an artificial harbour. Work began in 1845 on the construction of a massive breakwater sheltering a deepwater harbour adjacent to the Plain of St Nicolas. The construction of the Nouveau Port permitted the reclamation of the waterfront area and the creation of the vast Place St Nicolas, the largest open space in Bastia. Construction work on the port continued until the close of the century, by which time it had been connected (via a tunnel) to the railway system which was opened in 1888. The new road and the reclamation works made possible the urban development of the area of low-lying land between the new port and the railway line, marking a decisive stage in the expansion of the town away from its original site in Terra Nova and around the Vieux Port.

During the present century, three phases of growth, of differing speed and character, have taken place. Before the second World War, Bastia grew slowly, largely through the infilling of vacant land between the port and the railway terminal. The latter acted as a barrier to expansion westwards into the Fango valley but some ribbon development took place along the road to St Florent. War-time destruction led to a second period, of more rapid growth, during the immediate post-war period. Heavy bombing during the Liberation of October 1943 destroyed or severely damaged over 700 buildings, principally adjacent to the port. The residential rebuilding that was needed took the form of blocks of flats on the northern side of the town, effectively joining Bastia to the settlement of Toga; this area has subsequently functioned as a residential and light industrial suburb. The most recent expansion of the town is in the large residential complexes on the plain of Biguglia to the south. There the modern suburbs of Lupino and Bassanese, and the huge multi-storey apartment blocks of the Cité Aurore stand in stark contrast to the remainder of the town. North of Bastia, the steep hillsides of Cap Corse have checked growth in that direction, though an intermittent ribbon development of villas links Bastia to Erbalunga, ten kilometres along the coast. For the first time in its history, the expansion of the town has turned decisively southwards, a trend which is becoming more and more emphatic as new building sites mushroom on formerly agricultural land on the Biguglia Plain.

The linear pattern of growth summarised above was imposed by a site chosen as a fortress rather than for an agglomeration of over 50,000 inhabitants; this circumstance gives rise now to many problems. The commercial services and institutions of the town remain rooted about the axis of the Boulevard Paoli and in Terra Vecchia while the residential areas have moved progressively further away to north and south. To a greater extent than any other Corsican town, Bastia has established substantial suburbs from which there is a daily influx into the town centre, to work, social services and shops, along roads and streets that very readily become congested.

By virtue of its complex history, Bastia now possesses numerous distinctive zones that are characterised by specific functions, architectural forms and atmosphere. While lacking in real beauty and in certain areas—notably Terra Vecchia and the Citadelle—suffering from the need for physical renewal, much of the appeal of Bastia lies in the possibility of walking through a rapid succession of contrasted neighbourhoods, each the scene of different activities and with its own personality.

Such an itinerary might well begin at the Place St Nicolas, the geographical and social centre of the town. This is a handsome open space, bordered by shady avenues of plane trees and palms. To the east, the square overlooks the new port, animated by the movements of ferry boats to the continent, and to landward the Boulevard Général-de-Gaulle, with the town's principal restaurants and cafés. The charm of the Place St Nicolas derives from its function as a rendezvous, whether for small groups at midday for an apéritif or a casual games of *boules*, or at dusk for the *promenade*. The latter, a typical feature of Mediterranean towns, is particularly impressive by virtue of the large numbers who assemble and its formal informality. Custom and convention still persist in that the townsfolk take their evening stroll as family groups, often involving three generations, but the atmosphere is totally informal as friends greet acquaintances, review the day and pass on to another group.

To the east and north of the Place St Nicolas, the scene is dominated by transport in various forms. The new port is enclosed by an immense breakwater, the Jetée du Large, almost a kilometre long, which provides an excellent walk, combining a view of the port activity with a magnificent panorama of the town, Cap Corse, and the mountain ranges behind Bastia. Between the new port and the railway station runs the Avenue du Maréchal Sebastiani, on which are located the termini of many long-distance bus companies, numerous travel agencies, the post office, the railway station and several hotels catering for transient visitors. This street presents an interesting study in the contact between town and country, as buses from as far afield as Porto-Vecchio, Solenzara and Bonifacio unload sombre-clad peasants from the villages en route.

Altogether different in character is the main artery of the modern town, the Boulevard Paoli. A kilometre in length, it runs northwards from the Palais de Justice. The street is undistinguished architecturally, but is very animated, being the principal business and shopping district of the town. Here are to be found the main banks, offices and department stores, intermingled with small souvenir shops, book shops and cafés. In the adjacent Rue César-Campinchi, is the municipal theatre, badly damaged in 1943 and still (1970) in the process of being rebuilt.

South of the Place St Nicolas is one of the most distinctive and quaint parts of the town, the Terra Vecchia. The quaintness is in some measure diminished by the obvious signs of physical decay which mark the neighbourhood. Here the houses reach enormous heights—often up to eight storeys—but the ground floor is frequently occupied by some form of commerce, including some highly specialised craft and artisan activities. The Terra Vecchia also possesses the best ecclesiastical architecture in Bastia in the seventeenth-century churches of St Roch and St Jean-Baptiste. The latter is built in baroque style and contains impressive marble and stucco work. The twin towers of St Jean-Baptiste overlook the centre of Terra Vecchia, the Place de l'Hôtel de Ville, in which the daily open market is the most colourful aspect of the urban scene.

Terra Vecchia forms the northern flank of the *quartier* of the Vieux Port. Long since abandoned by commercial vessels, the Vieux Port is now used by fishing boats and pleasure craft. The harbour is sheltered by the Môle Genois and the Jetée du Dragon, from both of which there are magnificent views of the port and its impressive skyline. A broad *quai* follows the shore of the port from which steep narrow streets and staircases climb to the modern town. The view from the breakwaters is beyond doubt the most attractive landscape in the town, embracing the Citadelle, the port and the façade of St Jean-Baptiste. The Citadelle is poised above the port on the summit of rocky outcrops exaggerated in height by the massive fortifications. Access may be gained to the Citadelle by a staircase through the attractive Jardin Romieu.

The Citadelle consists of two elements, its system of fortifications including the Governor's Palace, and its residential community. The Governor's Palace dates from 1378 and was the only fortified element of the Genoese town before the construction of the Citadelle walls between 1480 and 1521. The Palace contains much of architectural interest and also houses the Corsican Museum of Ethnography. The museum is a kaleidoscope of Corsica's history, folk-lore and natural history, and is of great interest to the casual tourist as well as to the serious scholar. In the lee of the fortified palace stands the main open square, the Place du Donjon, which terminates in a terrace giving a fine view over the entire town and seawards to the Tuscan Archipelago. The residential section of the Citadelle consists of a dense rectilinear network of narrow streets separating tall housing blocks. Compared with the bustle of the modern town, the Citadelle is an enclave in which tranquillity emanates from a closely knit community that contains a high proportion of elderly persons. The focal point of the communty is the church of Ste Marie, dating from 1495. The church contains an eighteenth-century silver statuette of the Assumption which is the centrepiece of a procession through the town in August on the feast of the Assumption.

Bastia gives a final impression of being a busy commercial town possessing a growing urban proletariat. The town has burst out from the confines of its original site and the Citadelle now stands almost forgotten, by-passed by the mainstream of activity. The town's most recent development spreads in uncontrolled fashion over the plain of Biguglia, undirected by any overall plan. New offices, shops, showrooms, new light industries and apartment blocks line the coast road towards the airport. This haphazard development has no focus or community structure as yet. The creation of a real subsidiary commercial and employment centre in the south of the agglomeration would relieve some of the mounting pressure on the centre of Bastia which might then recapture some of its past charm.

AJACCIO

The notorious rivalry between Ajaccio and Bastia reflects the contrasted personalities of the two towns. To term Bastia 'proletarian' and Ajaccio 'patrician' is an overstatement of this contrast, but does go some way towards characterising the difference in atmosphere. Whereas Bastia on the east coast faces Italy, with all that this has implied in terms of historical events and commercial contacts, Ajaccio on the west coast has no such specific external orientation, but is in fact better placed in relation to the land mass of the island to extend its influence inland.

The difference in atmosphere begins with the site. Whereas Bastia is aligned along a fairly straight unspectacular coastline, Ajaccio lies around a large bay which is in turn an embayment within the magnificent Gulf of Ajaccio. From the heart of the old town, Ajaccio has expanded eastwards in a sweeping semicircle to the Campo dell' Oro, the delta of the Gravone and Prunelli rivers. The town is built in a natural amphitheatre, enclosed by mountains that shelter it from the north winds.

The old core of the town is the cité, occupying a lowland promontory that forms a natural breakwater for the bay to the north-east. The cité has the classic structure, shared by Bonifacio, of a citadelle and an *Haute-Ville*. The citadelle occupies the extremity of the promontory and is separated from the Haute-Ville by artificial earthworks. The Haute-Ville, which was also heavily fortified by the Genoese, occupies the neck of the peninsula and was accessible by a single gate. External residential areas did not develop to any extent in Ajaccio and in the eighteenth century all the essential elements of the town were still encompassed within the walls. In 1801 the walls surrounding the cité were pulled down, and under the aegis of the First Consul, the future outlines of the town were established according to a deliberate plan. The west wall of the old town made way for the vast Place du Diamant, now the Place Charles-de-Gaulle. From this focal point two new arteries were established; the Cours Napoléon, running directly northwards parallel to the coast, and at right angles to it, the Cours Grandval. Near the intersection of these two roads a formal square was laid out, the present Place Maréchal Foch, running along the line of the north wall and linking the two new roads with the seafront. From the compact and constricted site within the walled cité, Ajaccio was thus given the freedom to expand north and west, and at the same time to establish a strong contact with the sea.

In the first half of the nineteenth century, emphasis was placed on the erection of civic buildings appropriate to the town's new-

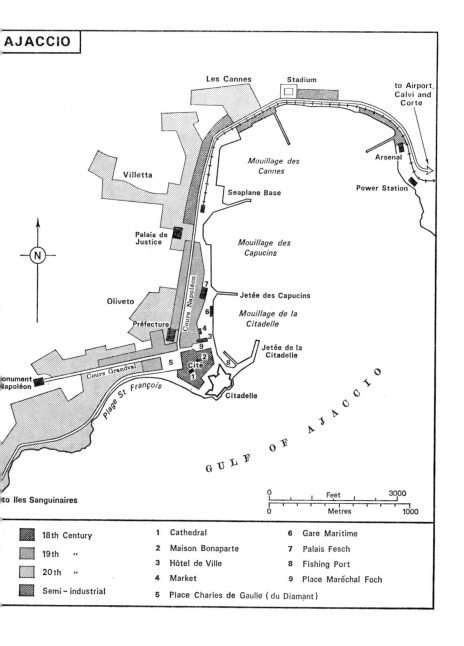

AJACCIO

▨ 18th Century	1 Cathedral	6 Gare Maritime	
▢ 19th "	2 Maison Bonaparte	7 Palais Fesch	
▨ 20th "	3 Hôtel de Ville	8 Fishing Port	
▨ Semi–industrial	4 Market	9 Place Maréchal Foch	
	5 Place Charles de Gaulle (du Diamant)		

found dignity as the island capital. From this period date the Hôtel de Ville, the Préfecture, the Palais Fesch and the municipal theatre. All these buildings were located to the north of the cité, and expansion to the west was much slower. The dominance of the northern tide of expansion was confirmed during the second half of the century with the construction of the port, the railway station and the growth of the Cours Napoléon as the main commercial artery of the town. Westward expansion continued to be hesitant and consisted of institutional buildings—schools, a hospital and the bishop's palace—interspersed with a few hotels. Residential development was restricted to prosperous detached houses and large open spaces were conserved.

The twentieth century has witnessed a continuation of the tentacular growth of the preceding century. A proliferation of semi-industrial activities now lines the waterfront from the railway station to the airport six kilometres away at Campo dell 'Oro. This includes petroleum storage, the abattoir, the power station, numerous depots and the military arsenal and seaplane base. As at Bastia, the most recent residential development has taken the form of large apartment complexes, built chiefly on the slopes behind the Cours Napoléon at Oliveto, less out of contact with the town than is the case of the Cité Aurore at Bastia. The ribbon development of villas on the shore of Cap Corse finds its counterpart at Ajaccio on the coast road along Plage St François towards the Iles Sanguinaires.

While an exploration of Bastia is an exercise in the discovery of the diverse character of the town, a walk through Ajaccio is essentially directed by the guidebook. Ajaccio has much more to offer of specifically tourist interest. Mention of only a few features serves to illustrate the resources of the town as a tourist attraction. The old town is a suitable starting point, both for its intrinsic interest and for the shrine of all tourists, the house in which Napoleon was born. The atmosphere of the cité is similar to that of the enclosed town at Bastia, with tall houses separated by narrow streets; these streets were built to fit the proportions of the sedan chair, in use until the nineteenth century, rather

Page 125 Ajaccio—a game of *boules* on the Place Charles-de-Gaulle

Page 126 Ajaccio—a view northeastwards across the Mouillage des Cannes and Mouillage des Capucins

than those of the automobile. The cathedral of Notre-Dame de la Miséricorde, built in 1554, has the form of a Greek cross and is surmounted by an imposing cupola.

Close by the cathedral is the Maison Bonaparte, where Napoleon was born on 15 August 1769. The house dates from the beginning of the seventeenth century and is now a public monument open to visitors and restored to its character at the time of Napoleon's residence there. The building was taken over by British soldiers during the occupation of Ajaccio in 1794, and ironically Napoleon's jailer on St Helena, Hudson Lowe, was housed there. At the extremity of the old cité, stands the Citadelle completed by the Genoese in 1559. The fortress is not open to visits but the Jetée de la Citadelle offers the best view over the whole town and a majestic panorama of the Gulf of Ajaccio. The breakwater shelters the small fishing harbour alongside the Quai Napoléon.

The cité is bordered to landward by two squares of markedly contrasted character. To the west, the Place Charles-de-Gaulle is a large open square planted with acacias and plane trees. Like Place St Nicolas in Bastia, it is favoured as a social rendezvous, offering views over the sea and the setting sun, and a vista of the old town with its cathedral and citadelle. To the north of the cité, Place Maréchal Foch is much smaller and altogether more stylish and intimate. It is richly lined with palms and plane trees and is graced by the fountain of the Quatre Lions over which stands a statue of Napoleon as First Consul. The square also contains a statuette of the Madonna, patron of the old cité. The Hôtel de Ville is situated on the square and is the site of the Musée Napoléonien, a comprehensive collection of paintings and sculptures of the Emperor and many of his relations. The charm of the square is enhanced by its juxtaposition with the old cité, the fishing port, and the colourful open market. It thus forms a natural social focus throughout the day, and compared with the busy Cours Napoléon, a haven of shade and calm.

The modern town has two main features, the commercial boulevard of the Cours Napoléon and the waterfront. In turn, the waterfront may be divided into two sections, north and south

н   127 of the Jetée des Capucins. To the south, the Mouillage de la Citadelle is used by fishing and pleasure craft and is also the terminus (Gare Maritime) of the ferry link to the continent. To the north, the Mouillage des Capucins shelters the commercial port and provides a spacious deep-water anchorage. The space between the Cours Napoléon and the waterfront is occupied by the main nineteenth-century residential quarter of the town, and also contains the Palais Fesch, the finest museum and art gallery in the island. This building comprises two features of interest, the Chapelle Impériale, which is the mausoleum of the Bonapartes including nine members of the family and in particular Napoleon's father, Charles, and his mother Letizia Ramolino, and the Musée Fesch. The latter is open to visitors and has a fine collection of Italian paintings spanning the fourteenth to eighteenth centuries, and a library containing rare books and manuscripts together with the most comprehensive collection of books relating to Corsica.

Ajaccio has a more prosperous and pleasing aspect than Bastia, with less evidence of decay at the core of the town and a fine setting between the sweep of the bay and the well-cultivated hill slopes, which contrast with the derelict fields surrounding Bastia. Ajaccio is punctuated with more open spaces, boulevards and public monuments and has suburban areas of style and quality; even the new housing estates blend into the urban landscape, unlike the anarchic sprawl of Bastia's latest expansion. There is, too, a greater atmosphere of sophistication and a more animated night life, stemming from the greater local importance of tourism and a higher proportion of professional and wealthy retired persons in the resident population. In short, the two towns are completely dissimilar and indeed there is little contact between them. The majority of the citizens of Ajaccio have probably never visited Bastia and vice versa, nor is there any obvious reason why they should. Thus the island's two largest towns maintain separate existences, practising a mutual disdain inherited from the past, reinforced by their physical settings and maintained by their different social and economic functions. The remaining towns are much smaller in size and status, and, apart from tourism, play a more localised role in the island's life.

CALVI

Calvi has approximately 3,000 inhabitants and has the status of a *sous-préfecture*. The town has a fine situation on the Gulf of Calvi, and this combined with a favoured climate, a picturesque townscape and good beaches, has made Calvi one of the most important tourist centres of the island. The town consists of two elements, the Citadelle containing the Haute-Ville and the *marine* or Basse-Ville. The citadelle surmounts a rocky promontory surveying the whole town and dominating the gulf. As at Bastia, it used to enclose both the Governor's Palace and a substantial community. The maze of narrow streets lends a picturesque atmosphere to the Haute-Ville but this is tinged with a sense of decay stemming from the age and derelict condition of some of the buildings. Tradition maintains that here Christopher Columbus was born in 1441, but this is an honour disputed with Genoa. The fortified Haute-Ville was a Genoese creation and the earlier settlement nearby was, as at Bastia, merely a small anchorage where the present Basse-Ville now stands.

The Genoese foundation dates from 1268 and occupied a special position in the republic's system of control of the island. The population of medieval Calvi was in large measure composed of Genoese settlers and was granted special privileges in respect of property and commerce, which ensured the loyalty of the town to the Genoese cause, even in opposition to the patriot Paoli.

The Basse-Ville covers a much greater area than does the enclosed town and its main feature of interest is the *marine*. Bordered by a broad quay, this is the most agreeable part of the town, combining a façade of old houses, hotels and cafés, the spectacle of fishing and pleasure craft at anchor or plying the bay, and, looming over all, the ramparts of the citadelle. The marine is continued southwards along the coast by a ribbon of tourist amenities, holiday camps, camping sites, villas and clubs set in *pinèdes*. In the summer season, Calvi is perhaps the most animated resort in the island and the tourist activity there is still expanding. On the south-west side of the town, the forts of Toretta and Mozello stand on an eminence which commands the finest view not only of the whole town but also of the high mountain ranges of the interior—and, on exceptionally clear days, of the Maritime Alps behind Nice, a prospect of 180 kilometres.

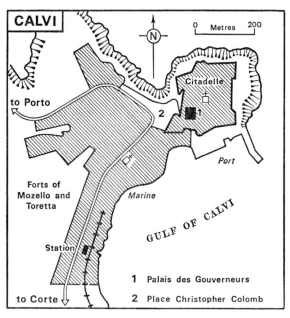

The future of Calvi is clearly as a tourist centre, and apart from serving a newly reclaimed agricultural area to the south, farmed by repatriates from Algeria, the town has little contact with the surrounding rural area. The airport, six kilometres south-east of Calvi, receives a growing number of tourists on inclusive tours and the town is a major staging point for itinerant holidaymakers.

Unlike any other Corsican town, Calvi has urban neighbours nearby in Calenzana and l'Ile-Rousse. Calenzana, fourteen kilometres inland to the south-east, is essentially an agricultural centre, situated where the fertile valleys of the Balagne meet the high mountains of the Monte Grosso range. As emphatically Corsican as Calvi was Genoese, Calenzana is nowadays a typical shepherd town of the interior, with some importance as a centre of wine production. The population numbers only about 1,500. L'Ile-Rousse, on the other hand, shares with Calvi a dependence on tourism. The town takes its name from a group of red granite islands which shelter a small harbour. Created by Paoli in opposition to the Genoese-dominated Calvi, l'Ile-Rousse has prospered in recent years through the growth of tourism and as the principal marketing centre for the wines and fruit of the Balagne. The town is so far less developed than Calvi, its expansion consisting of holiday villas rather than large tourist complexes, but its prospect for further development is undeniable—and inevitable.

SARTÈNE

Prosper Mérimée termed Sartène the most Corsican of all Corsican towns, and indeed it has perhaps retained more of its original character than any other town in the island. Sartène has few remarkable buildings; the entire mass of the settlement blends into the granite hillside on which it is built, giving a rather stern and ominous appearance that accords well with its troubled past. Sartène experienced repeated attacks by Moorish pirates and, when security from sea attack was assured, the town fell under the sway of the vendetta, with feuds taking place not only between families, but also between entire *quartiers* of the town. Above all, the old Sartène was an expression of the traditional society, its prominent citizens being the aristocratic heads of patriarchal families. Genoese influence was here at a minimum and Sartène was turned in on itself, aloof and mysterious rather than open to the outside world. The modern town has retained this atmosphere, epitomised in the strange procession of the *Catenacciu* each Good Friday.

The population of the town is now little more than 4,000 and appears to be declining. Sartène is the most important centre of wine making in the island but has been less affected by tourism

131

than the other towns, having neither rail nor air access. Its interest to the visitor resides not in physical attraction but as an expression of Corsican history, tradition and folk-lore. Its appeal is therefore to the informed connoisseur of the traditional Corsica, its language, tragedies and struggles, rather than to the casual tourist. Sartène lies much closer to the true spirit of Corsica than do the Genoese foundations or the twentieth-century tourist centres.

CORTE

Corte shares with Sartène a relationship to the traditional economic system of the interior but in other respects the two towns are very dissimilar. Whereas Sartène is remote, isolated and introspective, Corte is situated at a crossroads and a natural focal point. Ironically, with modern improvements in the island's communications, Corte has lost some of its importance as a regional centre. As the island has become more and more dependent on oversea connections, so the ports have become the important centres of communications, leaving Corte in a vacuum as the surrounding agricultural economy declined.

Corte has played a noble role in the island's history and this is still manifest in the town's landscape. The majestic citadelle, at an altitude of 500 metres, rivals that of Bonifacio for the grandeur of its site. It symbolises Corte's past as a centre of resistance and is now appropriately occupied by the Foreign Legion. The old town clings to the steep slope below the citadelle, the slope emphasising the height of the buildings and especially of the church. The focus of the old town is the Place Paoli; this small square, dominated by a statue of the patriot, is a social gathering place and scene of the evening promenade.

Corte has expanded from the old town nucleus in several forms. The line of the commercial axis of the Cours Paoli is prolonged eastwards in new residential districts. Across the Tavignano, the area between the river and the railway station is the site of small-scale industries and depots, municipal buildings and also the extensive barracks of the Foreign Legion. In contrast to these

132

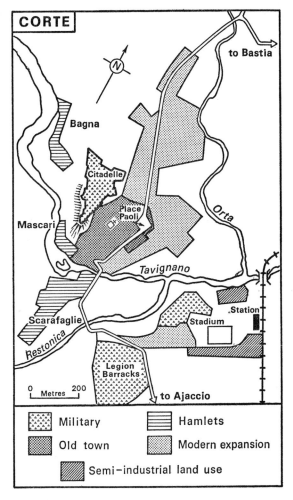

modern extensions, a different kind of settlement, the *paghliaghi*,
dates from a much earlier period. These are the hamlets of Bagna,
Scarafaglie and Mascari, which occupy the banks of the Tavignano close to the confluence with the Restonica. They are essentially agricultural settlements constituted by barns and livestock
stalls, introducing a purely rural aspect to the margin of the
town.

Corte has a population of approximately 5,000 and in spite of

133

the recent expansion of the agglomeration the population is tending to decline. This is due primarily to the weakening of its prime function as a regional centre for an exclusively agricultural hinterland. As the population of the surrounding mountainous rural area declines, so the importance of Corte as a service and marketing centre diminishes. Corte is however ideally qualified as a tourist centre. Apart from the intrinsic appeal of the citadelle and the town's association with Paoli, Corte is admirably placed for access to some of the most magnificent mountain scenery, notably the ascent of Monte Rotondo via the Restonica Gorges. Unfortunately, the growth of mountain holidays is greatly outdistanced by that of amenities in the coastal resorts. Much of Corte's tourist trade is thus derived from visitors *en passant* who include Corte on their itinerary rather than as a choice of holiday centre. Situated at the foot of great pine forests, Corte has great potential as a mountain resort for those appreciative of striking forest and mountain scenery, wildlife and tranquillity.

BONIFACIO

If Corte is situated at the heart of the island, then Bonifacio must surely be the most remote town of Corsica. Several features combine to make Bonifacio perhaps the most extraordinary town in the island. The setting is unique for Bonifacio is located in a highly distinctive region, the limestone plateau which forms the southern tip of the island and which faces Sardinia twelve kilometres distant. The dry surface of the plateau is dotted with *garrigue*, stunted shrubs adapted to the semi-arid conditions. The main productive land use consists of scattered vineyards and olive groves protected from the wind by high stone walls.

The town has approximately 2,300 inhabitants and its site outclasses even that of Corte as a spectacle. It is built on a narrow peninsula approximately 60 metres in height and 1,500m in length, overlooking the fjord-like Gulf of Bonifacio to the north and the Straits of Bonifacio to the south. Limestone cliffs drop precipitously from the town and are of an incredibly vivid whiteness. The town is divided into three sections by relief features and by artificial fortifications. The western half of the peninsula is occupied by the citadelle and was undoubtedly the original site of the settlement before this was moved further east by the Genoese in the thirteenth century. The citadelle is now a garrison of the Foreign Legion but may be visited by guide. It contains the town's most important church, the Eglise St Dominique built in the thirteenth and fourteenth centuries, and also commands fine views over the entrance to the Gulf of Bonifacio.

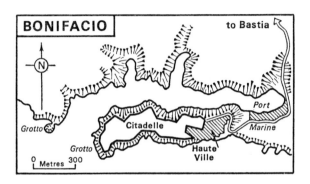

In the centre of the peninsula stands the Haute Ville, established by the Genoese and protected to landward by massive fortifications surmounting a steep slope. The town remained loyal to Genoa throughout the troubled centuries, resisting frequent attacks and sieges. The cramped site has resulted in narrow streets bordered by very tall buildings and the town can only be penetrated on foot. Magnificent views can be obtained from the fortifications and particularly from the terrace overlooking the overhanging cliffs which delimit the town to the south. The third element of the town lies outside the walls at sea level on the northern shore of the neck of the peninsula. This is the *marine*, site of the port from which the ferry sails to Sardinia and from where excursions depart to visit the marine grottoes around the Gulf of Bonifacio. The port is also a centre for shell fishing and in recent years a modest amount of expansion has taken place from the *marine* along the road towards Porto-Vecchio.

Although remote, Bonifacio is not isolated, for it is connected by road to Porto-Vecchio 27km to the north, and to Sartène, 54km to the north-west. By these routes come great numbers of tourists in the summer months, for the combination of natural features with the attractiveness of the town makes Bonifacio one of the showpieces of the island.

7   CORSICA ON THE MOVE

I SLANDS enjoy a certain mystique that is denied a mainland
location. There is an added dimension to travel to an island
absent from a simple overland journey. This romanticised
image, exploited in the tourist brochure, has a reverse side, for
insularity also exacts an economic price. Since the mid-nineteenth
century insularity has excluded Corsica from the vital economic
currents which have transformed mainland Europe and which
have laid bare the economy to outside competition. Improvements in transport connections had the double effect of permitting
the import of commodities that were better and cheaper than
those produced on the island, and also provided the routes by
which the exodus of population could take place. The economic
penalty of being an island is perpetuated in the present day in
that imported goods bear the cost of additional transport, as
compared with the mainland prices, while the Corsican products
are handicapped in like manner when they are marketed outside
the island. At present the level of exports is little more than one-
sixth the tonnage of imports.

There is a high volume of movement between Corsica and
the mainland, amounting in 1968 to over a million and a half
passengers and over 800,000 tons of freight for inward and outward movements together. Setting aside the tourist traffic, this
high level of movement is a measure of the island's economic
weakness. It reflects the dependence on imported foodstuffs, consumer goods and raw materials, and includes the movements
back and forth of expatriate Corsicans who still regard the island
as their home but who cannot find a livelihood there. It also
includes 4,000 young people who must seek their higher education outside the island.

Added to the problems of insularity *vis-à-vis* the outside world, are those of isolation within the island. Villages that are closely adjacent may be linked only by poor tracks, these being sufficient for the limited amount of social intercourse that occurs between rural communities. Even in the present day, rural dwellers may be better informed about Paris, which intrudes via the transistor radio, or the Côte d'Azur, described by workers holidaying in their natal villages, than about a settlement a mere dozen miles away over the mountains.

CORSICA AND LE CONTINENT

To the Corsican, mainland France is always *le continent*. To speak of the mainland as 'France' would be to imply that Corsica was something less than French. It is also a term used pejoratively to refer to a way of life different from and, in most Corsican eyes, inferior to that of the island.

The transport connections with the mainland are indispensable lifelines and their present shortcomings constitute one of the most commonly voiced grievances in the island.

Sea transport

Until the post-war period, external connections depended very heavily on maritime services. The journey was slow, schedules were infrequent during winter, and the conditions on board lacked in comfort for the ordinary passenger. Since 1948, the passenger service between mainland France and the island has been the monopoly of the Compagnie Générale Transatlantique. In return for the monopoly of the services from Marseilles and Nice to Bastia and Ajaccio, the company maintains a year-round service even though passenger traffic is less than profitable in the winter months. The journey time between Marseilles and Ajaccio is approximately nine hours, and between Nice and Bastia seven and a half hours, although the night crossings usually operate a slower schedule in order to give convenient disembarkation times. The same company operates services, largely seasonal in character, from Nice to Calvi and l'Ile-Rousse, and from Marseilles to Propriano. Services are also run on a modest scale between Toulon and Corsica in summer.

Since the late 1950s the growth of tourism has stimulated a considerable re-equipment of the 'Transat's' Corsica service. The first entirely new vessel, predictably named *Napoléon*, entered service in 1960, followed in 1962 by a second car ferry, the *Fred Scamaroni*. Subsequently the *Comté de Nice* and the *Corse* joined the service. The roll on-roll off facilities of these modern ferries have not only permitted the passage of an increased number of tourists and their vehicles, but have also inaugurated the transfer of loaded lorries and palletised cargo. In addition to the car ferries, the company also operates two modern freighters, the *Esterel* and the *Monte Cinto*, and three small cargo vessels. Cargo transport is not a monopoly and the Compagnie Méridionale de Navigation operates services from Marseilles to Ajaccio, Bastia and Calvi, as well as to the minor ports of l'Ile-Rousse, Propriano, Porto-Vecchio and Bonifacio. The refrigerated vessels, also equipped for the bulk carrying of wine, open the Corsican market to highly perishable goods.

A network of shipping services also links Bastia with mainland Italy, the Tuscan archipelago and Sardinia. The most important service is the Corsica Line link between Bastia and Genoa operated by the *Corsica Express*, and other connections are with Leghorn and with La Maddalena and Porto Torres on the northern coast of Sardinia. Portoferraio, on the island of Elba, is linked with Bastia by both conventional vessel and by hydrofoil. In addition, a ferry operates between Bonifacio and Santa Teresa, the nearest point in Sardinia, the crossing taking only one hour. Besides these fairly comprehensive scheduled services, Corsican ports have visits from cruising liners. Over 20,000 cruise passengers visit the island each year.

Ironically it is Bastia, with its much inferior harbour conditions, which greatly outweighs the fine natural harbour of Ajaccio in the volume of port activity. The commercial port of Bastia is an entirely artificial creation, with breakwaters built out on to a shallow marine shelf. By contrast, Ajaccio has a natural harbour in the form of a gulf approached by deep channels. Whereas Bastia is limited to vessels well below 10,000 tons, Ajaccio was able to accommodate the liner *France*, over 60,000 tons, on a visit during the celebrations of the bicentenary of Napoleon's birth in 1969. The harbour limitations of Bastia are offset by its strategic position for participation in the trade network of the Tyrrhenian Sea. Bastia too surpasses Ajaccio in the quality of its port hinterland. It has the larger population and a more populous, productive and accessible surrounding region. In one respect, however, Ajaccio retains a superiority. It is able to accommodate larger petroleum tankers, which discharge to storage tanks beside the bay. Petroleum has to be transferred overland to Bastia, and this is one of the vital arguments for the retention of the railway system, for when the road over the Col de Vizzavona is snow-blocked, the rail link remains open. This argument would disappear if a project to build a sea pipeline and terminal south of Bastia, allowing large tankers to discharge offshore, comes to fruition.

Superficially Corsica's maritime connections appear to be good, for the network is comprehensive and the vessels are modern. The improvements in the services have resulted very largely from the rapid growth of tourism and ironically this too is the main reason for the deficiencies of the service. Full services are restricted to the summer months, and at this period the ships are congested and early booking is necessary to ensure a crossing; the continued expansion of tourism will require additions to the fleet of vessels. By contrast, in winter the services are reduced and the vessels are operated well below capacity. Inevitably, the congestion in summer leads to frustration over reservation difficulties, while the lack of passenger traffic in winter, and also of adequate return freight traffic, makes the Corsica service expensive to operate. These are the major complaints about the services and the lack of competition is often held to be responsible for the high fares. It is difficult to see how, with an anomalous seasonal pattern of traffic and the need to amortise massive investment in new vessels, fares could be reduced without a substantial government subsidy. Such financial aid has been sought as a natural right ever since Corsica's attachment to France in order to integrate the island into the nation, but so far to no avail.

Air transport

Corsica has a long history of air transport, dating from the days of the flying boat service from Marseilles, via the seaplane base at Aspreto on the Gulf of Ajaccio, to the colonies in North Africa. After the last war, Ajaccio and Bastia were convenient staging and refuelling stops for Air France piston-engined air liners on the North African run. The introduction of Caravelle jet aircraft in 1959, coinciding with Corsica's growing popularity for tourists, transformed the significance of air travel. In 1969, for the first time, more passengers were handled by the island's two main airports, Bastia and Ajaccio, than by the maritime links. Handling almost 300,000 passengers a year, Bastia airport, once a small aerodrome known chiefly for its connection with Antoine de Saint-Exupéry's last tragic flight, is now the sixth ranking airport of France.

The principal scheduled services are operated by Air France and Air Inter, from Paris, Marseilles and Nice to Bastia and Ajaccio. Using Boeing and Caravelle jets, these services bring the island within one hour forty minutes of Paris, fifty minutes of Marseilles, and forty minutes of Nice. Summer services are operated into Calvi's smaller airport by propeller aircraft. In addition to these scheduled services, there has been a great increase in the number of charter services, mainly by jet aircraft in connection with inclusive tours from Britain and Germany. More recently still, internal services by light aircraft have been operated during the summer season. The Corsair company operates links between Bastia, Calvi, Ajaccio and Propriano. Air Alpes operates similar services with extensions to Chambéry, in the Savoy Alps, and to Olbia, in Sardinia. An Italian company, Aeralpi, flies a summer service from Rome to Bastia via Elba. While such services are as yet experimental and their economic viability uncertain, the first results have been encouraging.

Symptomatic of the growth of light aircraft transport is the opening to private users of the military air base of Solenzara, which in 1969 accounted for 8,000 private passengers. A further innovation has been the introduction of air car ferries, pioneered by the Compagnie Air Transport, using Bristol Superfreighters. This has developed into the *Flèche Corse*, a service which combines the rail link from Paris to Nîmes with connecting car ferry flights to Calvi and Bastia, operated by converted DC4 aircraft.

There seems little doubt that air travel is likely to figure more and more prominently in the pattern of movement between the island and the mainland in the future. The main developments anticipated are the upgrading of Calvi airport to accept more modern aircraft and the improvement of the minor airports, such as Propriano, which figure in the internal seasonal services and are increasingly used by private aircraft. The Corsicans have accepted the revolution in air travel with aplomb. The main employment centres of Corsican émigrés, Marseilles and the Riviera, have been brought within an hour of the island, and whether for leisure or business, the Parisian can reach the island in under two hours. Air travel has thus brought Corsica geographically closer to the continent, but at the same time there is a poignant contrast between the jet-age world of Bastia's modern airport and the decayed villages and deserted mountainsides only a few kilometres away.

The recent statistics of passenger and freight traffic are testament that, whatever the deficiencies of the transport systems, the island is no backwater as far as external communication is concerned. Indeed, in every respect, the external transport links exceed, in quality and efficiency, the provisions for circulation within the island.

THE RAILWAY SYSTEM

Corsica is served by 232 kilometres of railway line and the system must rank as one of the most spectacular in the world, both for

Page 143 *(above) Corsica Express,* the car ferry between Bastia and Genoa in Bastia harbour; *(below)* diesel unit of the Corsican Railways

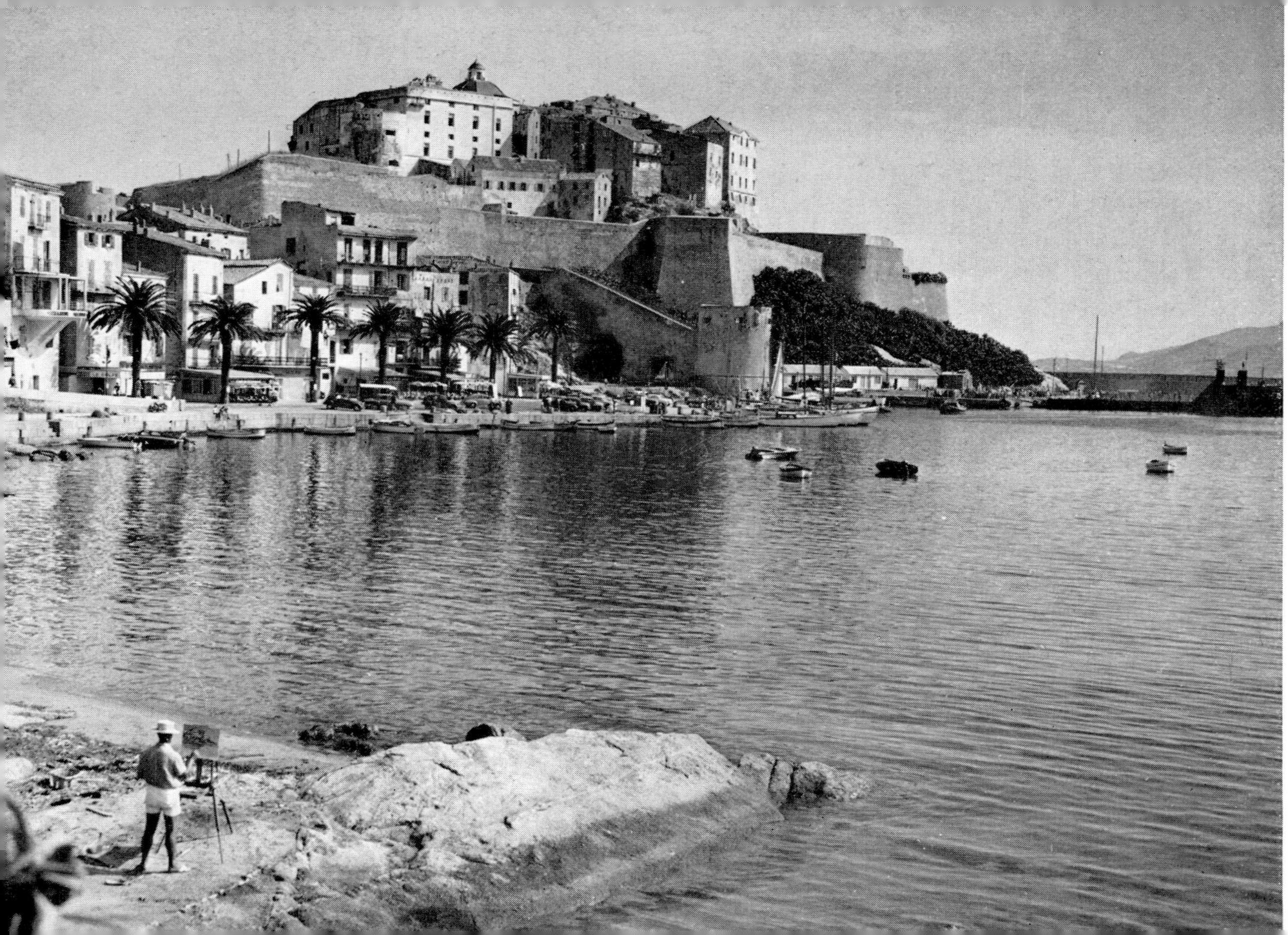

Page 144 Calvi—the citadelle over-looking the *marine*

the wildness of the scenery it traverses and for the engineering works that this has necessitated.

The construction dates from the end of the nineteenth century and was completed by stages. In 1888, Bastia was linked to Casamozza, near the mouth of the Golo, at which point a junction was built. The main line followed the Golo valley to Ponte-Leccia and thence to Corte while a second line continued southwards along the coastal plain to Ghisonaccia. In 1890 a spur was opened from Ponte-Leccia to Calvi, and in 1894 the most difficult section to engineer, from Corte to Ajaccio across the mountain spine of the island, was completed. Further construction was delayed by the first World War, but by 1939 the east coast route had been extended to Porto-Vecchio. It had been projected to extend this line to Bonifacio but when war broke out this link was incomplete. Heavy damage during the second World War, particularly the blowing up of bridges to prevent troop movements, rang the death knell of the east coast line. A short spur of ten kilometres, from Casamozza to Folleli, was maintained in operation until 1953, but at that date the east coast route south of Casamozza was abandoned. The network was thus reduced from its maximum length of 362 kilometres to its present length. In 1965, the nationalised railway company, the SNCF, conceded the system to private operation, the Chemins de Fer de la Corse, with headquarters at Bastia.

The present-day network consists essentially of one main line, running a distance of 158 kilometres from Bastia to Ajaccio via Corte, and a branch line from Ponte-Leccia to Calvi, a distance of 74 kilometres. The system is metre gauge and is single tracked with the exception of a limited number of stations used as passing points. Motive power is provided by diesel railcar units, usually hauling a second carriage. The journey between Bastia and Ajaccio takes three hours forty-five minutes, with a frequency of three services per day and with connecting services to Calvi. The service is one class only and many stations are merely halts at which the train stops only if flagged down. With the exception of the coastal section from Bastia to Casamozza, the entire route is scenically magnificent. The track crosses and recrosses ravines, describes huge curves on the steeper gradients, and offers a continuous panorama of mountain scenery. Particularly striking are the Golo valley, the whole of the Calvi branch line, and the climb to the Col de Vizzavona from Corte. This last section includes the spectacular passage of the Vecchio gorges, the traverse through the beech and pine forest of Vizzavona, and a superb view of the south face of Monte d'Oro.

Corsica's railway operates at a deficit and the reasons are not difficult to find. The routes traverse sparsely populated countryside and the stations are frequently several kilometres distant from the villages they serve. The degree of social and economic contact between Bastia and Ajaccio is comparatively small. Both towns are served by their own port and airport and are thus largely independent of each other. Further reasons for the railway's economic deficit are the highly seasonal nature of passenger traffic, and the high cost of track maintenance over mountainous terrain that is subject to severe winter conditions. The number of passengers carried in a year averages only 155,000, and freight averages 13,000 tons.

The arguments in favour of retaining the system are its undoubted appeal and utility for tourists and its function as a lifeline in winter when the high road passes are snow-blocked. The access to magnificent scenery and the friendly informality of the service are both of great appeal to the visitor. There is no doubt that closure, which is frequently threatened, would be a great loss to the interest of the island. Improvements in the road system and the development of internal air services could call into question the survival of the railway, especially when expensive re-equipment or major engineering works become essential. There is no doubt too that closure would be a loaded political issue, as evidence of yet further neglect of the island. Until the alternative means of transport have been improved, the railway has a role to play but unfortunately the laws of economics are not on its side.

THE ROAD SYSTEM

Each year, the *Rallye Corse*, the island version of the Monte Carlo and usually titled the 'race of 20,000 bends', takes place over a mountain circuit. It is safe to say that driving in Corsica represents almost continuous participation in such a test of skill and endurance.

In relation to its area and terrain, Corsica is in fact remarkably well served by roads. There are 2,000 kilometres of *routes nationales* which are well surfaced, 2,200 kilometres of *routes départementales* of varying quality, and 1,800 kilometres of *routes communales*. The difficulties of the road system are the inevitable preponderance of curves and hairpins, even on the main roads, the adverse driving conditions in winter, and the slow rate of travel that is compatible with safety.

The main axis of road transport is the N193 from Ajaccio to Bastia via Corte which follows generally the same route as the railway. The longest main road is the N198 from Bastia to Bonifacio. Following the coastal plain, this is the island's straightest and most direct road. Calvi and Bastia are linked via l'Ile-Rousse and St Florent by the N199 which continues to Ajaccio, along a serpentine route hugging the coast for much of its length. Ajaccio is linked to Sartène and Bonifacio by an even more difficult cross-country route.

From these main inter-urban routes, secondary roads diverge to serve the smaller centres and the tourist areas. Thus Cap Corse is served by a peripheral circuit running almost at sea level, the Castagniccia is easily explored via Morosaglia and Piedicroce and the Niolo is traversed via Calacuccia and the Col de Vergio to Evisa and Porto. The quality of the local roads, the *routes communales*, which include roughly surfaced forest roads, is often very poor, many villages being reached by steeply graded and badly surfaced roads. The road connections between adjacent villages are often very circuitous and it is at this local level that isolation, through the inadequacy of communications, is most commonly felt.

A good network of bus services operates between the main towns, but the frequency of operation is usually low. The principal year-round services are between Bastia and Ajaccio via Corte, between Bastia and Bonifacio via Porto-Vecchio and between Ajaccio and Bonifacio via Sartène. In addition most large villages have local services to the nearest town. The bus services are usually inconvenient for the visitor because of their timing. The tendency is for services to depart from rural areas very early in the morning and to return from the main towns in the evening, whereas a reverse pattern would generally be more appropriate to the needs of the visitor based on the larger centres. The tourist has nevertheless a large number of bus excursions at his disposal, departing mainly from Ajaccio, Bastia and Calvi.

With over 35,000 private vehicles registered on the island, the level of car ownership is surprisingly high. To this must be added 650 buses while the total number of lorries and vans registered exceeds 12,000. These figures show that the Corsican has accepted 'motorisation' as eagerly as his mainland fellow countryman, and several social consequences result from this fact. For the first time Corsica now has a significant number of rural-urban commuters, travelling daily from distant villages into Bastia and Ajaccio. Even that most traditional aspect of the rural economy, the migration of livestock herds between the mountains and coast, has been partially motorised. The transport of livestock in lorries makes for a more rapid movement over longer distances and a reduction in the Homeric scene of the herds migrating on the hoof and tended by their shepherds. The construction work on large dams in the valleys has introduced vehicles and machinery of a size never before seen in the interior and often manifestly exceeding the capacity of the roads. Finally, and most significantly in terms of changing social values, that most Mediterranean of customs, the evening *passegiata*, the *promenade du soir*, is becoming motorised, at least in the main towns. No longer do all the young people promenade; they cruise in small cars or on scooters, calling out to their comrades in the street as they drive round and round, reproducing on wheels the perambulation formerly made on foot. In combination with evening shopping, the motorised *passegiata* now makes the streets of Bastia as congested at eight in the evening as at the height of the day.

Corsicans are nowadays mobile to a greater exent than ever before, but it must be stressed that external connections have improved more rapidly than those within the island, and that much of interior Corsica still finds itself isolated. The inhabitant of Bastia or Ajaccio can fly to Nice in less time than a rural dweller in the interior might take to reach a neighbouring village.

8 AN ISLAND CULTURE

THE geographical integrity of an island might be expected to preserve the purity of its indigeous culture. An earlier chapter has shown, however, that for Corsica insularity has been but a feeble defence against outside influence and control. Over the centuries, the island has received and assimilated a multitude of external influences, and if those emanating from Italy and France have been the strongest, they have by no means excluded other cultural influences. As in many other islands, associated with insularity is a certain aggressive assertion of the indigenous nature of the culture, enriched rather than created by the diffusion of ideas and technology from outside. The battle lines are thus clearly drawn between those who would assert that virtually everything worthwhile in Corsica's cultural heritage has been derived from external sources, and those who would prefer to emphasise the importance and continuity of indigenous traditions. On the one hand, one can point to the Pisan churches and Genoese citadelles as representing the only outstanding architecture in the island. Equally well, the defender of indigenous culture can point to the legends, folk-lore and songs as being strong indications of a specifically Corsican culture, all the more authentic because of its reliance on oral tradition. Nowhere does this distinction between external influence and specifically Corsican evolution become so subtly blurred, and in academic circles, so contentiously disputed, as in the case of the Corsican language. This therefore forms a good starting point from which to enter the debate as to whether an island culture exists in its own right, or simply as a result of an accretion of varied cultures deposited in one of Europe's backyards.

CORSE—LANGUAGE OR PATOIS?

The speaking of Corse has a significance beyond that of communication, it is a symbol of the island's distinctiveness. Whether spoken within the island or among the colonies of Corsicans on the mainland, the speech exerts a bonding influence. However, it is difficult to resolve the question as to whether Corse is a language in its own right or simply a patois, a localised variation of the Tuscan dialect of Italian. It has certain of the features which distinguish a discrete language, for example the numerous variations in local dialect which characterise most live languages. It has also a formation from numerous sources, superimposed in successive layers from very early times. On the other hand, Corse has no defined alphabet, no dictionary, and no completely agreed rules of grammar. Corse must be regarded as something more than a patois, but something less than a language.

Certain facts can be established without much ambiguity. For example Latin accounts for the root of rather more than 60 per cent of the words employed in Corse. It is reasonable to seek an origin for these in the six centuries of Roman rule but it must be remembered that Romanisation was effective only on the fringes of the island, and the survival of pre-Roman vocabulary in present-day speech may be ascribed to the failure of Roman civilisation to penetrate into the interior of the island. Moreover, the Roman rule was succeeded by five centuries of barbarism, during which the survival of Latin was only precariously maintained by the church. It now seems probable that the basic affinity with Latin came not directly but indirectly, from Italian, during the centuries of domination by Pisa and Genoa.

Throughout the Pisan and Genoese periods, Italian became the language of commerce and administration, and there is substantial evidence that the Corsicans achieved considerable fluency in it. Boswell, writing in 1765 of his travels on the island, observed that Italian was spoken with greater purity there than in many regions of the Italian peninsula. However, proficiency in Italian was a feature of the commercial classes, the coastal areas, and

151

specifically the ports. In the interior, the introduction of Italian speech was more limited. Penetration was achieved by commerce, by the establishment of garrisons and in the course of military campaigns. Nor was Italian always assimilated in pure form. The predominantly Tuscan manner of speech was variegated by the regional dialects of mercenary soldiers drawn from different parts of the peninsula. The isolation of the interior, where self-sufficient economies and a higher degree of autonomy in everyday life prevailed, permitted older forms of speech to continue. In the absence of a literature, the survival of archaic speech depended entirely on an oral tradition. Corse was acquired in the cradle from lullabies, developed through children's rhymes and games, enriched by the relating of legends, and, all too characteristically, perfected by the sound of the *lamenti*, the *ballate*, and the *voceri*, associated with battles or doleful events.

French replaced Italian as the official language after the annexation, but it has had surprisingly little impact on Corse. It is only on the continent that the Corsicans have adopted hybrid expressions of French and Corse. Unlike the Tuscan dialect, which progressively infiltrated into the more ancient language to form the present composite speech of Corse, French has been adopted as a parallel but separate language. The position now is that French is universally spoken and understood; it is the language of instruction in schools, and of commerce and administration. Italian has virtually disappeared from use, the more so after the hostilities and occupation during the second World War, but it is still widely understood because of its close relationship to Corse.

Corse is still widely used and fulfils several functions. Throughout the more traditional regions of the island, Corse is still the everyday means of communication. On a wider scale, it remains the language of familiarity and intimacy between families and groups of friends, as opposed to the French they use in the course of their occupations. It is the language of the bars and cafés, the games of cards and *boules*, the witty political jibes, and the evening *passegiata*, especially amongst the older generation. Corse is more formally employed in the folk-lore, festivities and religious ceremonies of the island, the chief fund of preservation being the repertoire of song which accompanies such functions. Last of all, the island language forms a field of scholarly investigation, the chief objective of which is its preservation by giving literary expression to its oral tradition. This activity has been a matter of some controversy in the present century. In part this stems inevitably from the attempt to codify and transliterate an immensely complex speech, in which opportunities for differences of scholarly interpretation are only too abundant. More seriously, for a period after 1921, the maintenance of the language became associated with a movement for political autonomy. The controversy surrounding the language question, a controversy it must be stressed which affects only a small minority of the population, has had the unfortunate effect of proliferating a large number of reviews and bulletins, each too ephemeral to provide optimum conditions for a flourishing literature to develop. A few periodicals, and notably *U Muntese*, appear in Corse, and a number of reviews devoted to poetry, history and folk-lore also continue, but Corse remains supremely a language of the people, little read, very little written, but still widely spoken.

No summary description of Corse speech may be attempted. It defies simple generalisation beyond noting the basic affinity with the Tuscan dialect of Italian. There are, however, major differences of pronunciation as compared with Italian which may be alluded to. The 'o' vowel sound tends to be transformed into 'u', and the 'e' into the shorter 'i' sound. Monte Cinto thus becomes 'Monti Cintu' in Corse. Likewise the pronunciation of consonants and the positioning of stress vary considerably from Italian.

There is significant variation of dialect within the island. It has been customary to distinguish between the *langue du Nord*, spoken in the north and north-east, and the *langue du Sud*, spoken south of a line roughly from Sagone to Porto-Vecchio. The northern dialect has the closer affinity with Tuscan, reflecting its open vowels and lilting rhythm. In the south, there is greater affinity with the dialect of Sardinia, with its harsher con-

153

sonants and heavier rhythm. The lilting quality of 'll' is expressed in the south by 'dd' or 'dh'. The proportion of Latin words diminishes in the south, with a greater frequency of Arabic and Spanish roots. This division into two main dialects is a gross oversimplification, as up to a dozen local dialects may exist, although the boundaries between them remain imprecise. The best-developed examples are the dialects of Ajaccio, and more particularly, that of Bonifacio. The dialect of Bonifacio is highly distinctive and differs most widely from the more 'standard' speech of the north-east.

Corse must be regarded as a linguistic hybrid which, although basically derived from Latin, retains a significant amount of speech with no relationship to Romance language. This element derives in part from the pre-Latin speech of the indigenous population, on to which has been grafted an admixture of foreign vocabulary brought about by commercial contacts, with Greece and Carthage for example, and conflict with barbarian groups, notably the Moors. Denied the consolidation that a literary tradition would have provided, the survival of Corse is consonant with the island's general resistance to suppression throughout its history. Its future survival is almost certainly better assured through the oral tradition than by the valiant attempts of etymologists to standardise a written form. The speech is under threat however by virtue both of the depopulation of the most traditional regions of the island and of the appearance of the 'generation gap' with increasing urbanisation. The young people of the island have discovered alternatives to the old heroes. The exploits of patriots and bandits, both real and legendary, are fading before the idols of the cinema, the sporting fraternity and the world of pop music. To the urban teenager, Corse is associated with a dying economy, while French, and even more so *Franglais* and pseudo-American slang, are the languages of wider horizons and greater opportunities which only begin outside the island.

It would be ironical if, by the time the grammarians, etymologists and lexicographers have completed their work, they should have defined a language almost as dead as the Latin from which it in large measure derives. For the moment no such crisis exists but progress customarily exacts a heavy price of fragile cultures. One is led to the conclusion that whereas it is probably true that much of the island's past, which weighs heavily on the Corsican temperament and 'soul', can perhaps only be adequately expressed in Corse, it is also probably true that the progress being made in the towns, resorts, hydro-electric and irrigation schemes can find expression only in French and other international languages.

ARCHITECTURE

Whether language or patois, Corse is something special to the island and an undeniable element in Corsican culture. In the sphere of architecture, however, nowhere are the dependence on external inspiration and effort and the modesty of the Corsican contribution more apparent.

Indigenous Corsican architecture is characterised by its simplicity, functional design and massive form. The troubled history of the island has imposed a preoccupation with security which has outweighed almost all aesthetic considerations. The emphasis on security characterises even domestic architecture in village and town alike. The construction of individual dwellings on top of each other in buildings often six or seven storeys high, entered by a single doorway that was frequently accessible only from an external stairway, was an expression of the desire for security. New building thus tended to grow by vertical accretion on top of massive foundations, themselves commonly built on the ruins of a previous building. If the villages of Corsica stand out so boldly in the landscape, this results as much from the high average height of buildings as from the strategic hilltop locations favoured for their sites.

In the towns, the constriction of the space within the perimeter of the citadelles and the limited area of settlement permitted outside the walls by the Genoese governors account for the incredible height of town dwellings. This is seen to best effect in the Vieux Port of Bastia, where the natural slope emphasises the effect of

155

height, and at Bonifacio, where the buildings appear to be a continuation of the perpendicular face of the cliffs.

Outside the urban and rural agglomerations, the stark simplicity of indigenous architecture is symbolised by the shepherds' huts, and even more in the shelters of the mountain pastures which resemble pyramids of heaped stone. The Corsican is not by nature a builder of any pretension. Obliged for the most part to work with extremely hard rock, finesse in masonry has been less valued than ease of construction and repair, and external appearance sacrificed to solidarity and durability. In a history punctuated by pillage and destruction, the incentive to erect fine buildings has been conspicuously absent. Similarly, traditional economies that required a maximum of effort to ensure survival and, in the case of pastoralism, a migratory basis to life, left few hands idle to fashion buildings and few minds free to explore and innovate architectural style. In only one instance has skill in masonry, if not aesthetic taste, evolved and that significantly attaches to reverence for the dead. More effort and skill have been applied to the mausoleums and tombs of the dead than to the residences of the living. Nor have the Corsicans displayed until recently much interest in the preservation of their architectural heritage. Many of their finest monuments, especially the military fortifications and watchtowers, have been allowed to decay. While many ruins are legitimate evidence of heroic battles, others are symptomatic of past neglect and even deliberate destruction for the sake of acquiring building materials.

It cannot be denied that the total effect of many Corsican settlements is often impressive when viewed against their natural setting. The massiveness of aspect blends with the mountain backcloth and the simplicity of style is in natural accord with the primitive economic activities. All too often, however, closer inspection reveals the sores of abandoned houses and a general aura of dereliction, at least in external appearance. To find fine architecture we must look for the buildings left behind by Corsica's erstwhile masters. Of these, the works of the Greeks and Romans remain only in vestigial form. Relics of Greek, but more particularly, Roman building are to be found at Aleria. Remains are even more vestigial in the case of the Roman town of Mariana near the mouth of the Golo.

These are examples of architecture in an academic sense, for nothing remains of the construction other than the outline of their plans. The value is archaeological rather than architectural and greater interest attaches to the ceramics, coins and utensils displayed at the museums of Aleria and Bastia. To find buildings of architectural merit still standing, it is necessary to pass beyond the shadowy centuries of the barbarian invasions into the eleventh century when the island fell under Pisan control. In the ensuing seven centuries of Italian domination, initially by Pisa and for much longer by Genoa, two forms of architecture developed which are still characteristic features of the landscape; Pisan ecclesiastical building and Genoese military constructions.

Pisan ecclesiastical architecture established a pattern in church building that was followed throughout succeeding centuries with little change until the baroque period. The Pisan church style was essentially that of the Romanesque basilica, a rectangular building with parallel central colonnades and terminating in a semi-circular apse. Pisan influence was strongest in the northeast and it is here that the greatest concentration of early Pisan churches, as opposed to the later copies, are to be found. Ironically, the two finest examples of Pisan architecture, the oldest buildings in the island, stand in isolation, their settlements having long since disappeared. These two churches, the Canonica of Mariana and the cathedral of Nebbio, are characterised by extreme simplicity of style and plan. The Canonica dates from the early twelfth century and now stands in almost total isolation near the airport of Bastia. The town of Mariana was obliterated by successive barbarian attacks and the malarial condition of the lowland precluded a permanent resettling of the site. The restoration of the church in 1931 has preserved Corsica's oldest and finest building and it is undeniably the prototype of the Pisan ecclesiastical style. The cathedral of Nebbio, built in the thirteenth century, has the same plan and dimensions (some 30 metres by

157

12 metres) as the Canonica, but there is some evolution in detail. The white limestone and the greater external decoration give a lighter appearance.

Several other churches were built in the thirteenth century, notably the fine example at St Michel de Murato, 20 kilometres south-west of Bastia. The subsequent spread of church building throughout the Genoese period witnessed some slight evolution in detail but the essential simplicity of the Romanesque form remained unchanged. The main developments concerned the interior ornamentation, with stucco work, elaborate high altars and carvings, testifying more to the extravagance of Corsican piety than to aesthetic advance. The gothic style virtually by-passed the island completely, as if the Pisan style, with its simplicity of construction, corresponded most closely to the limited aspirations of the Corsicans as builders.

No major innovation occurred until the end of the fifteenth century when imitation of the classical Italian baroque style became apparent. The best examples are to be found in Bastia in the citadelle church of Ste Marie and the more imposing St Jean-Baptiste overlooking the Vieux Port. The more effusive external design and the garish extravagance of the interiors form the strongest possible contrast with the clean outlines of the Pisan style.

Corsica can thus claim little originality in ecclesiastical architecture, the island's own contribution being limited to the embellishment of styles acquired directly from Italy. Apart from obvious contrasts in scale, church architecture has a high degree of uniformity. By contrast, the military architecture derived from the Genoese occupation offers a much greater diversity, if only because the detail of construction had to be accommodated to varying local topographical conditions. To the Genoese, Corsica owes its majestic citadelles which form the kernels of most of its towns, a large number of coastal watchtowers, and a much smaller number of bridges on strategic military routes.

The defensive system created by the Genoese involved three main elements, citadelles, fortresses and watchtowers. The citadelles enclosed the Genoese settlements with their governor's palace and also guarded anchorages or ports. These citadelles formed the nuclei of Bastia, Ajaccio, Calvi, St Florent, Porto-Vecchio and Bonifacio. The citadelle of Calvi may be considered the most successful expression of military architecture in terms of the blending of natural and artificial fortifications. That of Bonifacio was the most extensive and complex, and by virtue of its site, almost impregnable. At intervals between the citadelle strongholds, smaller coastal fortresses acted as garrison stations and refuges during campaigns. Examples are Algajola in the Balagne, Aleria, and Girolata, the last on an embayment in the Gulf of Porto. The defensive system was completed by watch-towers punctuating the entire coastline and built principally during the sixteenth century in response to raiding by Moorish corsairs. Almost 150 were built and were used as beacons to warn of the approach of a hostile fleet—it is considered that the chain was capable of flashing a warning around the island in the space of an hour.

As compared with earlier square Pisan towers, as at Toga, Nonza and Porto, the Genoese towers were invariably round-based and conical in shape. Thirty to fifty feet in height, the towers accommodated a lookout watch who gained access by an external ladder which was then lifted inside as a defence measure. They served to warn adjacent villages of attack but only a few were sufficiently large to act as refuges for the villagers. By the nature of their function, the towers were prone to destruction in attack and to subsequent dilapidation and vandalism. As a result their number has been greatly diminished over the centuries. Most are now in ruins, but as a step towards their preservation private individuals have recently been encouraged to rent them. On condition that their original exterior appearance is restored, their interiors can be converted to present-day functions. The Genoese bridges characteristically have a hump-back form, called in Corse *u ponti di spina-cavaddu,* bridges with a back like a horse. The best example is the triple-arched bridge at Ponte-Leccia, and six or seven less imposing bridges are still in use.

Paradoxically the French, with their centuries of architectural glory and their modern technological skill, have done little to enhance the architecture of the island in almost two centuries of rule. Exception made perhaps of the Chapelle Impériale at Ajaccio, which houses the tombs of several of the Bonaparte family, the French contribution has been in engineering more than in ecclesiastical or secular architecture. In the nineteenth century, the construction of the railway system necessitated the building of many fine bridges and viaducts. In the twentieth century the major achievements have been in the construction of dams. In other respects contemporary architecture has been less than inspired. The low-cost, high-density apartment complexes which disfigure the fringes of most French towns have burgeoned in Ajaccio and Bastia, on sites deserving more imaginative development. With a few notable exceptions, the growth of tourism has inevitably stimulated building of an 'instant' kind and strictly functional aspect.

In short, we cannot offer convincing evidence of an island culture in the buildings of Corsica. Native building showed little inclination to develop beyond what was strictly practical and secure. Corsica was content to accept an 'off the peg' ecclesiastical style from Pisa, simple to emulate, as was the late-renaissance baroque style adopted at a later date. It is paradoxical that the two aspects of life closest to the Corsican *esprit*, religious devotion and involvement in combat, should be enacted in buildings constructed or inspired by outsiders.

While Corsica has comparatively few great buildings, it cannot be denied that the island has several combinations of buildings and natural site which achieve great beauty. The examples of Calvi, Corte and Bonifacio are in this sense outstanding.

FOLK-LORE

If the material features of the landscape offer no expression of a specifically Corsican culture, it follows that we must turn to man himself, and to expressions of the mentality, temperament

Page 161 The citadelle of Corte, perched high above the town

Page 162 Bonifacio—a Genoese stronghold on the limestone cliffs at Corsica's southern tip. The steps cut in the cliff face are known as the King of Aragon's staircase

and soul of the islanders. This offers more promising ground for it leads into the spheres of folk-lore, traditions, religion and superstition, fields which are fertile in observable facts and intangible emotions in roughly equal proportions.

In most islands which have succumbed to tourist invasion, folk-lore has become part of the industry, a synthetic, instant quaintness dispossessed of much of its original meaning. This is not yet the case in Corsica, for although traditional songs are featured in a handful of clubs in the summer resorts, in large part folk-lore remains part of the indigenous culture. The absence of commercial contamination, with the notable exception of the cult of Napoleon, is possibly explained by the predominantly tragic content. A folk-lore deeply imbued with a preoccupation with warfare and death, offers lugubrious fare for the holiday-maker seeking romance and escape from unpleasant reality. In both the spiritual and lay folk-lore of Corsica, the element of fiesta and rejoicing is overshadowed by the evocation of suffering. Only the vendetta and banditry have acquired—largely erroneously— some semblance of romance in the popular imagination.

It is difficult to define the boundaries of folk-lore but a liberal interpretation permits discussion of all aspects of the island's traditional life as expressed in custom, song, religion and superstition. The preoccupation with death, usually of a violent character, has been alluded to, and nowhere is this more evident and more inaccurately interpreted by the outsider than in the case of the vendetta and banditry.

The vendetta and banditry

The word *vendetta*, from the Latin root *vindicta* meaning vengeance, is the chief, and perhaps only, contribution of Corsica to international vocabulary. The vendetta has come to be symbolised through the novels of Prosper Mérimée, *Mateo Falcone* and *Columba*, as a matter of revenge for the sake of outraged honour. This is an oversimplified view, for in its time the vendetta has been both better and worse than this. Intially the vendetta arose as a form of instant justice exacted by vigilantes at a time

K

163

when official justice was non-existent, slow or corrupt. The roots of the vendetta thus go back into the troubled centuries of the medieval times, when death, whether from disease, outside attack or inter-clan rivalry was so commonplace as to become an accepted part of life. Recourse to impartial justice being unavailable, the vendetta represented a spontaneous judgement in which any miscarriage was subsequently resolved by reciprocal murder by the offended party.

Until the Genoese intervention, the vendetta was strictly a domestic affair, an honourable means of resolving feuds between families and clans. The main disadvantage was not that the course of justice was prejudiced, for no effective alternative existed, but rather that it prevented a permanent unifying of interests in opposition to outside aggressors. Corsica was to pay a high price for the generations of mistrust, intrigue and bloodshed. Under Genoese incitement, the vendetta degenerated both in its scale and motivation, for the custom offered ideal conditions to exploit the principle of 'divide and rule'. The repressive measures of the Bank of St George, especially in the extortion of taxes under duress, made the prospect of natural justice seem even more remote. In response, the Corsicans resorted to their own summary forms of justice. Estimates of the scale of murder committed in the name of justice vary widely, but a total of 30,000 in the latter Genoese period may not be exaggerated. More importantly, political intrigue and economic gain became more important motivations than affronts to honour, and the vendetta declined from its former honourable traditions into a more sordid power struggle within the island.

The vendetta principle survived the French annexation on a much reduced basis, although still accounting for over one hundred murders each year. Most such murders were attributable to sexual jealousies, election rivalries and disputes over grazing land and water. The isolation of villages and the resultant social claustrophobia undoubtedly provided conditions where petty jealousies and minor misdemeanours took on a heightened significance.

The practice of banditry, another Corsican tradition of some antiquity, was related to the vendetta in that bandits were fugitives from official justice who took to the maquis and forest with the connivance and support of their families. The exploits of many such fugitives are immortalised in legends, but after 1918 banditry assumed a more criminally organised form. Robbery and the extortion of tribute and protection money persisted until they were stamped out by para-military operations in the early 1930s. Similarly the vendetta, in its original form, is no longer of social significance on the island. Sporadic murders revive echoes of the vendetta but are usually more mundane than the vengeance of affronted honour. Typical incidents involve disputes between the youths who have remained in their villages as shepherds and farmers, and the youths who return from the continent, bearing external signs of prosperity and acquired sophistication, sufficient to turn the heads of the village girls. That such petty incidents should lead to violence springs from another Corsican characteristic, a love of firearms and an insistence, even among young people, on carrying them about as a symbol of status and self-assertiveness. It seems clear that the ubiquity of arms, coupled with a naturally dramatic temperament easily inflamed by strong alcohol, accounts for the more spectacular incidents which shake the calm of Corsican village life at infrequent intervals. Trivial incidents can thus escalate to the ultimate crime with little or no premeditation.

The Corsican's inherited penchant for violent action and contempt for official law has largely passed out of the island's life by transference to the continent. Corsicans form a significant element in the *milieu*, the French underworld, particularly in Marseilles and on the Riviera. The origin of this is not difficult to appreciate, in the arrival of jobless Corsicans in a large cosmopolitan port city that has a long history of criminal activity. If a Corsican emigrant becomes recruited to the underworld, it becomes a simple matter to call in members of the family or village acquaintances from the island. Circumstances like these are favourable bases for professional gang development, with specialisation in prostitution and drug peddling in particular. The association of gangs derived from specific villages or families has enabled a sordid form of the vendetta to continue when the criminal activities of rival gangs come into conflict. A new aristocracy, albeit shadowy, in the tradition of the island's bandits, has grown up on the mainland. The fact remains that these leaders of the underworld retain a permanent interest, often almost philanthropical, in their home villages, bestowing gifts on good causes and supporting their favoured political faction. Their criminal activities are however firmly fixed outside Corsica, for by comparison the pickings to be made from the island would be lean indeed.

Religion and superstition

It may seem profane to classify religion under the heading of folk-lore but the boundary between orthodoxy and superstition is not always clear. Moreover, it is in the religious festivals that much of the genuine folk-lore of the island finds its richest expression.

Corsica has remained solidly attached to the Roman Catholic faith throughout its history. At the height of the barbarian attacks it was to the Papacy that the island turned for protection and it was in convents that the famous *consultes* were held, Théodore de Neuhoff was crowned king, and Pascal Paoli proclaimed the island's independence. A *consulte* held at Corte in 1735 placed the island under the protection of the Immaculate Conception, a status institutionalised in the island's anthem *Dio vi salvi Regina*. As its emblem, the self-styled republic adopted the *Tête de More*, the head of a Moor blindfolded before Christian decapitation. The lifting of the blindfold in the emblem supposedly testifies to the more enlightened character of Paoli's regime. The whole island, and Ajaccio in particular, is dedicated to veneration of Our Lady.

The chief exception to complete Roman orthodoxy was brought about by the founding of a Greek colony in 1676 at Paomia near Cargese. The Greeks came as refugees, under the aegis of the

Genoese, from Turkish oppression in the Mani peninsula of the Peloponnisos. The prosperity of this and nearby Greek refugee settlements evoked the anger of the Corsican population and led to their destruction. Taking refuge in Ajaccio, the Greek population was not resettled until after the French annexation. In 1774, the village of Cargese was built to accommodate the refugees and a Greek Uniate church erected. The Greek population is now generally assimilated but has remained faithful to its Uniate rite.

The borderline between religion and superstition and folk-lore is particularly ill defined in the case of religious legend. The case may be cited of the martyrdom in the fourth century of Ste Julie de Nonza. Refusing to deny her faith, she was crucified and her breasts were cut off. Where they were cast down, two springs miraculously appeared. The cult is perpetuated at Nonza in the dedication of the sixteenth-century church and in the celebration of her feast day on 22 May, while beside the church, the fountain of Ste Julie is reputed to have miraculous healing powers.

The preoccupation of the Corsican mind with death finds its ultimate expression in religion, and it is during the passion celebrations of Holy Week that religious folk-lore reaches its peak. Virtually every parish has its particular form of celebration, but several ceremonies are outstanding for the numbers that they attract, the fervour attached to them, and the traditional ritual. Most famed is the *Catenacciu of Sartène*, so named after the chained penitent who represents the living Christ. The procession is held on the night of Good Friday, and the central figure is the *Grand Pénitent*, a hooded figure dressed in red robes, carrying a huge cross and dragging heavy chains. The identity of the chief penitent is known only to the priest and a waiting list extends years ahead for this key role in the passion play. Behind the *Grand Pénitent* follows the *Petit Pénitent*, dressed in white and also of concealed identity, who plays the role of Simon of Cyrene, aiding Christ to carry the cross. The cross is followed by eight other hooded penitents bearing a statue with broken limbs and symbolising the dead Christ. The procession is accompanied by an animated crowd, hustling the *Catenacciu* in an attempt to make him fall and reveal his identity. By virtue of the long waiting list, the *Catenacciu* is commonly elderly, and his falls, portraying Christ's stumblings on the route to Calvary, are as much a result of carrying a heavy burden through narrow streets and up steep staircases and of being jostled by the crowd as of a deliberate enactment. The singing which accompanies the procession has a macabre quality, resembling shouting rather than song. When the procession reaches the main square the priest blesses the crowd in the name of the dead Christ and the ceremony is ended.

The procession of the *Catenacciu* and the accompanying chants are of medieval origin and until quite recently the spectacle had a more vigorous character. The suffering endured by the figure of Christ formerly made it an appropriate role for a criminal, who received the abuse and buffets of the crowd. It is also believed that at times bandits filled the role as a form of expiation of their misdemeanours, thus increasing the efforts of the crowd to reveal the identity of the chief penitent. The ceremony has lost some of its past severity and drama but it is fitting that this most impressive and mystical folk-lore should survive in Sartène, Corsica's most traditional town.

Similar torchlight processions are held in Corte and Bonifacio. By contrast, those of Calvi have a lighter touch. The ceremonies begin on Holy Thursday with the blessing of the *canistrelli*, traditional Corsican cakes. On the night of Good Friday, hooded and barefoot penitents begin the procession from the parish church of Ste Marie, near the port, to the cathedral church of St Jean-Baptiste in the citadelle. The procession is interrupted four times for the performance of the *granitola*, a complicated spiralling movement, the term meaning a snail.

These essentially urban processions contrast with the rural setting of the Good Friday ceremonies held in Brando commune, to the north of Bastia in Cap Corse. There the ceremonies begin in the morning with the *Cerca*, the search. Processions set out from all the constituent hamlets of the commune, such as Erba-

168

lunga on the coast, Pozzo, Silgaggia and Mausoleo, lost in the maquis slopes. The processions wind around for several kilometres, pausing at churches and chapels, before converging on the chapel of Notre Dame de Lavasina, the island's most sacred shrine. Here extreme piety is mingled with the enjoyment of a copious lunch in the company of friends from each of the settlements, the elderly folk in particular having been separated throughout the winter months. In the evening, a *granitola* is performed as a climax to the day's ceremonies.

In addition to the Easter celebrations most towns and villages celebrate the feast day of their patron saint as well as that of the Assumption of the Virgin on 15 August, a national holiday which by happy chance coincides with the birthdate of Napoleon. Veneration of the Virgin has special significance at Ajaccio, for Notre Dame de la Miséricorde is officially regarded as the town's protector. This tradition dates from the threat of plague in 1656, when the town council placed Ajaccio under the protection of Notre Dame. The town was spared the plague, whereupon the municipality established statutes defining Ajaccio's eternal dedication to the Virgin. This association is celebrated annually on 18 March with great enthusiasm. On the night of the 17th floodlit celebrations take place in the Place Foch, where the statue of the Madonna looks down from a marble niche. On the 18th, the municipality invites the Bishop to celebrate High Mass in the town's cathedral.

Religion and folk-lore find their finest expression in the festival held at Casamaccioli each September. This feast, marking the Nativity of the Virgin, is known as the *Santa della Stella* or *Santa di Niolo*. According to legend, in the early fifteenth century a ship was in danger of foundering in the Gulf of Galeria. The captain appealed to the Virgin for aid and a star appeared over a convent in the Filosorma valley. The ship was saved and in recognition the captain presented an image of the Madonna, the *Santa della Stella*, to the convent. A century later, the convent was sacked by marauding Turks and the faithful placed the statue on a mule, which traversed the Monte Cinto range unguided, finally stopping at Casamaccioli, a small hamlet outside Cala-cuccia, near the headwaters of the Golo river. Here a church was erected as a shrine for the statue of the Madonna, now named after the local region as the *Santa di Niolo.*

The feast is in fact a glorious mixture of piety, trading, tradi-tional folk-lore and unrestrained merrymaking, lasting three days and attracting thousands of participants. The setting of the feast is magnificent, on a wooded slope at the foot of Monte Cinto. The 8th of September is given over almost entirely to veneration of the *Santa,* with continuous religious services and the per-formance of a *granitola.* In comparison with the sombre associa-tions of the Good Friday celebrations, the feast of the *Santa di Niolo* is a joyful occasion, the processions being accompanied by fusillades shot into the air. The site of the outdoor celebrations is the *Campo,* a tree-shaded fairground. Here marquees are erected for refreshment, gambling and also competitions in oratory and poetry in the Corsican dialect. The feast traditionally brought together shepherds and naturally developed into an opportunity for trading. Held in the heart of Corsica, it still preserves the best features of traditional life in the island, com-bining the religious devotion of the pilgrims, the aura of legend and superstition, the continuation of the oral traditions of the language, and the secular traditions of the fair.

The examples of religious folk-lore which have been described are of course the high points in the religious year. On an every-day basis the pattern of religious observation is more subdued. While Sunday observance is more or less the norm, especially among the womenfolk, the priestly role is seen by the peasantry as a purely spiritual one. He is there to baptise the infants and to give extreme unction to the dying, but everyday matters are commonly regarded as none of his business. In the past everyday behaviour was guided as much by superstitions as by orthodox beliefs.

Some of these superstitions, especially those involving witch-craft, were deeply held convictions. Until recently, in the remoter villages of Corsica, belief in the ability of certain people—the *signadori*—to cast an evil eye or to make magic signs when possessed by a devil was common. Even more terrifying were the *mazzeri*, meaning 'killers'. At night the souls of the *mazzeri* were supposed to hunt, albeit involuntarily, the souls of living persons, dooming them to an early death. Worst of all were the *streghi*, the witches who were transformed into small animals and sucked the blood of infants. All these forms of witchcraft and sorcery were held to be possession of the soul by the devil during hours of sleep and the only remedy was to exorcise the demon as quickly as possible. Legends even extended to epic battles between the *mazzeri* and witches of a village with those of neighbouring villages, the favoured battlefields being the wild mountain passes. The isolated character, the wild scenery and the gloomy forests of such locations must clearly have held sufficient terror at night to impress the minds of simple people, making the most extravagant beliefs appear convincing.

The more bloodcurdling superstitions and fantasies no longer hold much force, but the village dweller nevertheless retains an awareness of his natural surroundings and their past significance as the haunts of supernatural beings. Improved education may have eliminated the more terrifying aspects of superstition, but among the older inhabitants memories remain of the times when belief in malevolent supernatural forces was commonplace and confidence in the healing property of white magic widespread.

Song, ancient and modern

Corsicans are natural singers and it is unlikely that any visitor to the island should not remark their talent and the pleasure they derive from singing. The songs that the tourist is most likely to hear are the romantic and sentimental ballads popularised since 1945 by the island's most popular idol of song, Tino Rossi. The accompaniment is invariably the guitar, the most widely played instrument in the island. Several night clubs specialise in traditional songs sung in Corse. In fact music permeates Corsican life at several levels, ranging from, at one extreme, the archaic *paghiella*, three-part singing by men preserved in certain villages, to the ever-increasing number of juke boxes at the other. Between these two extremes come the town and village bands which animate carnival parades, and the individual singer, quietly improvising on traditional refrains, singing for his own enjoyment and that of his friends while sitting outside cafés in the still of dusk.

Beneath the modern generally melodic and lilting manner of singing, reminiscent of Italian ballads, lies a much sterner indigenous tradition, associated as is so much of popular folk-lore with the cult of death. Apart from the shepherd, singing or playing the flute or pan pipes to while away the loneliness of his vigil, the chief exponents of traditional song were the women-folk. In consonance with the troubled times their songs were of warfare, death and vengeance. *Lamenti* were sung to accompany the menfolk departing for battle and *ballate* were sung at wakes held for the dead. Most characteristic were the *voceri* sung at the wake of a man who had suffered violent death and inciting the relatives to revenge. The *voceri* were led by a principal *voceratrice*, skilled in improvisation in verse to a traditional metre. Gathered round the bed of the deceased, the women sang in mournful chorus as the *voceratrice* extolled in song the main events of the dead man's life, while the menfolk sat in a separate room, reflecting on the departed over a quiet drink and smoke. The practice is now little observed outside the more remote pastoral villages and it is perhaps as well, for it recalls less happy days in the island's history. Singing in *paghiella* is nowadays even more uncommon and is limited to certain mountain communes where this tradition of male part-singing in Corse has persisted. The main examples are at Rusio, in the Castagniccia, and Sermano, near Corte, where on the chief feast days the mass is still sung *a paghiella*.

Of the remainder of Corsican culture and folk-lore little need be said. The island has produced few painters of fame and the principal Corsican writers produced their literature in French and lived outside the island. Indeed the best-known literature inspired by Corsica was from the pens of outsiders, as in the case

172

of Mérimée (*Mateo Falcone* and *Columba*), Alexandre Dumas (*The Corsican Brothers*), Alphonse Daudet (*Lettres de Mon Moulin*) and the *Voyages* of Flaubert. An account of the most stirring days in the island's history, the rebellion led by Paoli, has been immortalised by a British chronicler, Boswell. Artisan crafts formerly widespread, especially in the Castagniccia, now have little importance. Work in stone, iron and wood was always simple in style, as were textiles and pottery. Most of the trinketry that accompanies the tourist trade is imported and of no artistic merit. Some effort has been made to revive crafts, especially through village workshops in the Castagniccia, around Corte and in the Balagne. An important step in this direction was made with the establishment of *Cyrne Arte*, an artists' village founded in 1962 at Palasca near Belgodere in the Balagne. This aims to revive rural artisan crafts and to encourage young artists and sculptors. In total, the output of craft industries is still small and the design remains simple. To buy direct from workshops is the best guarantee that an article is indeed locally produced, and the discerning collector can find objects of merit especially in the form of carved stone or olive wood statuettes. Some of the more mundane aspects of traditional life, such as local costume and dances, have virtually disappeared and are preserved only by a handful of folk groups.

THE ISLAND CULTURE

We thus return to our original debate. Does Corsica possess its own island culture? If we write the word with a capital letter then the answer must be in the negative. Corsica has been too much involved in the power struggles of outside states to have escaped from strong external influences which were assimilated with only minor adjustment. Similarly the centuries of struggle against natural obstacles, against invaders, and against fellow Corsicans, produced a background of almost continuous insecurity which furnished a breed of warriors rather than of artists. Architectural styles thus reflect the designs and preferences of their

173

masters. The religious celebrations have much in common with those of Catholic Mediterranean Europe and it was only in little quirks and idiosyncracies that indigenous traits were expressed.

If we write culture with a small letter, taken to mean simply the pattern of everyday life in its traditional setting and with its attendant folk-lore, then Corsica can claim to have a separate personality. To find this identity we must leave the tourist beaches and the main towns, which are increasingly a twentieth-century façade behind which lies the Homeric Corsica, the land of the shepherd. Here, in its mountain enclaves, a dwindling population retains something of the timeless Corsica, living under the weight of a dolorous history and an ungenerous environment. Even here it is perhaps only a matter of time before what at present recalls a museum of traditional practices and attitudes is closed down room by room. Every year the maquis advances further, the forests become more damaged by fire and the outlying villages lose their populations. Corsica becomes more and more an urban community and the culture of towns is that of the mass media, the consumer society, and even in Corsica, extroverted, looking to outside markets, a cosmopolitan tourist clientèle, and largely turning its back on an interior, rich in history, splendid in the grandeur of its scenery, but incapable of supporting even its present meagre population.

9   ISLAND COMPENDIUM

A t the risk of seeming a catalogue, this final chapter groups together items of information which, however mundane may help the visitor to gain more interest from his stay in the island. For the armchair traveller, the same information may fill in details of the island's life omitted from the general themes of the earlier chapters. Apart from the books listed in the bibliography, detailed information is available from the French Government Tourist Office, 178 Piccadilly, London W1, and from the Maison de la Corse, 20 Rue de la Paix, Paris 1er. Once on the island, the Syndicats d'Initiative in the principal towns are invaluable sources of information.

ADMINISTRATION

As an integral part of France, Corsica is administered in exactly the same manner as the mainland *départements*. The capital, Ajaccio, is the seat of the Préfet, while Bastia, Corte, Calvi and Sartène are *sous-préfectures* and the capitals of *arrondissements*. Below this level, the island is divided into 62 cantons and 364 communes. Each commune has an elected mayor and a part-time secretary, usually the schoolmaster, who administer the day-to-day affairs of the commune. In view of the remoteness of the villages from larger towns, these local powers assume some importance and the position of mayor is a hotly contested political appointment. For the visitor, a visit to Corsica is in all essentials identical with one to mainland France, from the point of view of administration, political system and legal code. The visitor thus requires no special documents other than a valid passport. The monetary system is identical to that of the mainland and the main

175

banks are represented in the larger towns but are sparse and open for limited periods only in the countryside. Prices, particularly in the main tourist areas, tend to be a little higher than the average in mainland France, reflecting the additional cost of transport and the small proportion of home-produced articles.

TRAVEL AND ACCOMMODATION

The holiday season extends from May until the end of September, and many visitors may find the extremes of the season the most attractive. By May the maquis is in full aromatic bloom and the temperatures are comfortably warm without being oppressive. Similarly, late September and even early October offer pleasant weather. The advantages of the extremes of the season are the absence of crowds and reduced prices in some hotels and in travel charges. By contrast the high season offers ideal conditions for bathing, marine sports and climbing, a more lively night life and a greater range of organised excursions. The simplest, but most expensive, means of access is by air, from London or Paris. The air fare can be reduced by flying from Marseilles or Nice. The cheapest method of travel, and the only convenient means of transporting vehicles or camping equipment, is by boat from Marseilles, Nice or Genoa, and in summer, from Toulon. It is essential to make reservations on all forms of travel well in advance, and on some vessels reservation of couchettes is advisable for a night crossing.

There are approximately 170 classified hotels in the island of which about half are open all the year round. However, there is a heavy concentration of hotels in the limited number of towns and resorts, and many are small. Most of the newer hotels are of a high quality and consequently relatively expensive for a prolonged visit. From all points of view it is therefore desirable to reserve accommodation, at a fixed price, well in advance of a visit. A further hundred unclassified hotels offer more modest accommodation and boarding houses offer inexpensive rooms in the main towns. In the larger villages of the interior, accommodation is available in auberges and family houses. Amenities there are spartan but prices are low, hospitality is traditionally excellent and the arrangement is attractive for those who wish to get to know the real Corsica rather than the 'tourist traps'.

The holiday village system is burgeoning and offers a range of standards from luxury tourist complexes to simple bungalow sites. The prospective patron should ascertain the character of such village accommodation and also of its location. Many occupy delightful settings on unspoilt beaches but are distant from the main urban or tourist centres. The holiday village system offers many advantages, but it is important to ensure that the quality and location of the village correspond to the type of holiday envisaged.

At the bottom of the scale, in terms of expense but not necessarily in terms of appeal, there are over forty organised camp sites. These are located primarily at the coast but are also to be found in the interior. In addition, it is possible to camp in most of the state forests and virtually anywhere in the countryside. In the latter case, permission should be obtained from the mayor's office of the village and membership of a camping organisation is desirable. Particular care is called for when camping in the forests and prior permission should be obtained from the Conservation des Eaux et Forêts, 4 Boulevard Marcaggi, Ajaccio. The dangers of fire cannot be too highly stressed. With a rainless period often as long as two months in summer, the forest and maquis becomes a virtual tinder box. This sparsity of summer rainfall makes Corsica an ideal camping ground and enables the visitor to enjoy majestic scenery away from the crowded tourist centres. Respect for property, scrupulous care in the use of fire, and adequate warm clothing when camping at altitude, even in summer, are the only necessary precautions. Full details of camping sites and of all kinds of accommodation including category and prices are available from the Maison de la Corse, Paris and the French Government Tourist Office in London.

GASTRONOMY

Corsican tastes in food generally resemble those of southern France and Italy, but the island has in addition a number of traditional specialities—though these are not always easily obtained in restaurants. Much of the island's own produce— cheeses, charcuterie, game, fruit and wine—is widely available and of good quality. Among the specialities, the gourmet should seek *stufatu*, which is macaroni in a sauce of onions, mushrooms and cheese, or the more exotic delicacy of wild boar in wine and chestnut sauce. Blackbirds are prized for their flavour, derived from feeding on the wild berries of the maquis. They are eaten both roasted and as a pâté. Other traditional dishes are based on chestnut flour, eaten as fritters (*fiadonu*). Goat and kid meat forms the basis of many roasts and stews in the everyday diet in preference to more expensive beef and veal. Corsican charcuterie is appreciated for its distinctive flavour, the pigs often being fed on chestnuts while the smoking process uses the aromatic wood of the maquis. The best charcuterie includes *prisuttu*, a smoked raw ham, and *lonzu,* a rolled smoked fillet of pork, *coppa*, highly spiced pork shoulder, and the saucisson *salsiccie.*

The island's ewe flock supports production of good quality cheeses, which along with goats' milk cheese are available in most restaurants. Ewe's milk is made into a Roquefort type cheese, such as *bleu de Corse* or Ponte-Leccia for example, while *brocciu* is a white goat cheese used mainly in the preparation of savoury dishes. At the coast sea food dishes are abundant and varied, ranging from soups and *azimunu*, a bouillabaisse of several kinds of fish, to the more expensive lobsters. In the mountains, grilled trout is a delicacy found between March and September. Fresh fruit range from apricots and peaches to citrus fruits, especially mandarins. Candied cedrat is a delicacy and a survival of a once widely grown fruit. Cedrats are now used mainly for the production of liqueur.

In the hotels and main restaurants, the cuisine is international in response to the cosmopolitan clientèle, but even the most timid

Page 179 (left) Pisan architecture: St Michel de Murato; *(right)* baroque architecture: St Jean-Baptiste at Bastia

Page 180 Procession of the Feast of the Assumption, Ajaccio

palate should be tempted by Corsican charcuterie and cheeses as well as game dishes, fish and fruit. The locally produced wines and spirits can be recommended, although the amateur might well beware of the high alcohol content of the wine, commonly 12° and often as high as 15° proof. The most common ordinary wine, marketed mainly by co-operatives, is a rosé, but several villages and small regions produce high-quality wines with reputations beyond the confines of the island. The best examples are the white and rosé wines of Patrimonio, a village near St Florent, and the white muscats of Cap Corse, especially from Rogliano. The vineyards of Bastelicaccia, Peri and Cuttoli, near Ajaccio, produce good wines, and in the south the Tallano and Figari wines are strong and have a rich bouquet. A dozen other local wines are also exported and in general the quality is improving as production becomes more and more concentrated in well-equipped co-operatives with expert wine makers. In common with much of Mediterranean France, the customary apéritif is a *pastis*. The island variety *Casanis* is manufactured at Bastia. Spirits include *marc* and other *eaux-de-vie* produced from the berries of the maquis, notably myrtle and arbutus. The liqueur *Cédratine* is made from the cedrat fruit.

EDUCATION AND SOCIAL SERVICES

Corsica faces severe difficulties in providing and maintaining an adequate level of social service in view of the scattered distribution of the population in the interior and large sparsely inhabited areas. It has proved impossible to maintain a high density of expensive services for the benefit of very small local populations in rural Corsica. There is thus a heavy concentration of services in Ajaccio and Bastia while in the countryside social services are very thinly spread.

Both Ajaccio and Bastia possess two lycées and both have colleges of secondary and technical education, the latter concerned mainly with agricultural training. Corte and Sartène have lycées serving the centre and south of the island respectively. The

L

limited availability of grammar schools implies that rural children must enter schools in Bastia or Ajaccio as boarders. Because of the expense involved, many parents with children of high school age prefer to take a house and employment in the town. In some instances this move proves permanent and thus the problems of education in the interior is a further factor in rural depopulation. Calvi has a secondary modern school and twenty-nine other secondary modern schools are scattered throughout rural Corsica, each serving a wide catchment area. There are almost 450 primary schools in rural Corsica but the number is likely to decline both because of the difficulty of recruiting teachers and the diminishing number of pupils in the more remote areas. There is as yet no university and the island's 4,000 students must seek their higher education on the mainland. There is a popular demand for the establishment of a university as it is felt that this would help stem the 'brain drain' from the island. So far there is no indication that this demand will be fulfilled and the educational system remains under the tutelage of the University Academy of Nice.

Health services show an even greater concentration in the two largest towns. This is particularly the case with doctors and dentists who, being in liberal professions, have established practices in the more populous and lucrative areas. Thus Ajaccio has over one hundred doctors, Bastia sixty-five, and Calvi forty-one, while the whole of rural Corsica has under seventy. Outside the large towns there are only fourteen dentists and three registered midwives. Ajaccio, Bastia and Sartène have general hospitals and Corte has a cottage hospital. The problem in rural Corsica is not merely the lack of adequate facilities, but also of attracting qualified staff to areas where remuneration may be low and opportunities for appropriate social and professional contact limited.

THE PRESS

The daily press is dominated by Corsican editions of three regional newspapers flown in each morning from mainland France. The largest circulation is achieved by *Nice-Matin*, followed by *Le Provençal* and *La Marseillaise*. In each of these papers, two pages are devoted to island news and photographs supplied by agents in Corsica. The items are arranged under the headings of localities and include in addition to news reports such parochial items as births, deaths and marriages and notices of forthcoming events. The island editions of these newspapers are also widely read by émigré Corsicans in south-east France. Parisian evening papers are brought by air to the island each afternoon. There are now only three Corsican daily papers, one at Ajaccio and two at Bastia, with a small and essentially localised circulation.

WILDLIFE

There is a varied but unspectacular wildlife in the island, which appeals to the naturalist and the sportsman to a greater extent than to the casual visitor. Pride of place is taken in the animal kingdom by the *mouflon*, a wild, horned sheep, which is protected from hunting. It roams the crags and forests of the Cinto massif and the Bavella mountains. Much more widespread and enthusiastically hunted is the wild boar. The boar inhabits the forest and maquis and is particularly numerous in the south-west and in the Porto valley around Evisa. It is hunted in organised shoots with beaters in the season from September to January. Red deer are found in the Solenzara valley, and hares are widely hunted. There are several species of lizards and snakes, all harmless.

Greater interest for the naturalist attaches to the butterfly population. The prevalent flowering maquis vegetation offers an ideal habitat and although over 800 varieties of butterfly have been recorded it is certain that very many new discoveries remain to be made. The bird population is extremely rich, owing to Corsica's location on migration routes and to the variety of habitats, ranging from mountain crags, forest, and open maquis to lagoons and salt marshes. Bird life includes birds of prey, chiefly the buzzard, in the mountains, vast numbers of berry-eating birds

183

in the open maquis, together with migratory game birds, such as quail, woodcock and doves, and such marsh birds as duck, teal, snipe, grebe and curlew. The marsh hunting season lasts from the end of July until mid-February and game shooting including blackbirds and thrushes, from late August until early January.

Hunting is a major Corsican pastime and provides many of the island's traditional dishes. Conservation of wildlife is thus a serious problem not only because of the enthusiasm with which anything that moves is shot but also because of the damage done to habitats by forest and maquis fires. Visitors may obtain a licence for hunting for approximately sixty francs and details may be obtained from the Fédération Départementale des Chasseurs, 13 Boulevard François Salini, Ajaccio.

In contrast with the variety of animal and bird life, there are only two common species of freshwater fish, the trout and the eel. However, the abundance makes good the lack of variety. The trout season extends from the third week in February to mid-September, with best catches from March to June. Practically all the mountain streams have trout but the best centres are Corte, for the Tavignano, Restonica, Venaco and Vecchio rivers; Propriano, for the lower Rizzanese and Taravo rivers; Asco, for the Asco river; and Calacuccia for the upper Golo river. Other fine fishing rivers are the Fango, the Ficarella, both easily reached from Calvi, the Manganello, close by the mountain resort of Vizzavona, and the Solenzara. The lagoons of the east coast together with the in-shore waters shelter a bewildering variety of fish, molluscs and other marine life. The interest is not only for the fisherman but also for the undersea explorer. About 200 species of fish have been recorded, ranging from the eels and flat fish of the lagoons to the multitude of rock fish. A fishing licence costs about fourteen francs and details of locations and seasons can be obtained from the Fédération Départementale de Pêche et de Pisciculture, 7 Boulevard Paoli, Bastia. At St Florent there is a research centre of marine study and the main centres of undersea fishing are Calvi, Galeria, Ajaccio, Propriano, Porto-Vecchio and Cap Corse.

CORSICA'S GREATEST SON

Few visitors will leave Corsica unaware of the fact that it was the birthplace of one of the most illustrious men of history. In his brilliant collection of essays, Geoffrey Wagner goes so far as to portray the island temperament as an 'Emperor Complex', the manifestations of which are extreme pride and an exaggerated indifference to material and pecuniary matters. Whether the casual visitor will detect such imperious qualities is perhaps doubtful but more tangible evidence abounds that the island's greatest exile still holds an important position.

Physical reminders abound in Napoleon's natal town Ajaccio, the *cité impériale*. No fewer than three statues commemorate his exalted position. In the heart of the town, a statue of Napoleon as First Consul surmounts the fountain of the Quatre Lions in the Place Maréchal Foch. On the terrace of the Place de-Gaulle, an equestrian figure of the Emperor in Roman imperial costume gazes out to sea; the bronze statue surmounts a granite base at each corner of which are placed statues of his brothers, Joseph, Lucien, Louis and Jerôme. Even more impressive is the monument completed in 1938 which overlooks the Place Général Giraud, where the pedestal surmounts a huge stairway and the statue is of Napoleon in his great coat and *bicorne* hat in the classic pose, one arm thrust inside the coat. It is a replica of the statue in Les Invalides which formerly surmounted the Vendôme column. By contrast, Bastia is much less enthusiastically Bonapartist and a single statue shares the Place St Nicolas with the *Monument aux Morts* of the first World War. The white marble statue surrounded by palms depicts Napoleon in the dress of a Roman Emperor. Similarly, a single street, Rue Napoléon, commemorates the great man, whereas as in Ajaccio practically every other street bears his name, that of a member of his family or has some other Napoleonic association.

The Emperor features prominently in commercial life also. Countless establishments from the most distinguished hotel, the four-star Napoléon Bonaparte at l'Ile-Rousse, to the humblest bar,

185

have borrowed his name. The souvenir shops are full of articles (mass-produced outside the island) commemorating Napoleon. Metal busts, statuettes and plaques are ubiquitous, as are pottery and china bearing his head, initials or imperial eagle insignia. Such bric-à-brac rarely has artistic merit but, in an island where authentic souvenirs are difficult to find, provides a tolerable memento of the island before one boards the ferry boat *Napoléon* to return to the mainland.

On a less trivial plane, the island's association with the Bonaparte family is an important focus of interest for even the most casual student of history. In this context Ajaccio is the primary centre of attraction and visits to the Musée Napoléonien, the Maison Bonaparte and to the Chapelle Impériale in the Palais Fesch are essential. The cult of Napoleon attained a peak in 1969 with the celebration of the bicentenary of his birth. The occasion was marked by the issue of commemorative medals and stamps, a visit to the island by the liner *France* on an 'imperial cruise', and an oration at Ajaccio by the President of the Republic.

THE CORSICAN BANNER

After the head of Napoleon the next most commonly seen insignia in the island is the *Tête de More*, the Moor's head. This negroid head is in fact only the centrepiece of the much more elaborate heraldic arms of the island which date from a *consulte* held at Corte in 1762 presided over by Pascal Paoli. The central figure is the Moor's head bearing a ribbon over the forehead. This design is on an ornate shield, borne by two giant tritons, half-human, half-beast, which brandish clubs and are set in an assortment of marine and military emblems. The crest is surmounted by a royal crown. Prior to 1762, the emblem of the island had been the Virgin, symbolising the placing of the island under the protection of the Immaculate Conception by a *consulte* in 1735. In 1736, Théodore de Neuhoff placed the Virgin on the reverse side of his coinage and the Moor's head on the obverse side.

The origin and symbolism of the crest is much debated, for the various components antedate Paoli's *consulte*. It may date from the expulsion of the Saracens in the ninth century, in which case decapitation and the mounting of the head on a shield would have formed an appropriate trophy. More likely the emblem derives from the heraldic standard of the crusades and specifically from the Aragonese claim to the island in the thirteenth century. The Moor's head was originally blindfolded and it is believed that Paoli chose to raise the band to symbolise enlightenment.

The *Tête de More* is encountered daily, as a trade mark on various foods and wines, as a decoration on cards and journals and, as in the case of Napoleon, in trinkets and bric-à-brac for tourists. It remains Corsica's national emblem and, along with the island anthem, a symbol of pride and separate identity.

WHERE TO GO, WHAT TO SEE

As this book is not intended as a guide, this compendium seeks only to illustrate the range of attractions and opportunities which the island offers. The prospective visitor will be well rewarded by reference to Dorothy Carrington's excellent *This Corsica*, both for planning a visit and for a companion guide while on the island. The majority of visitors generally fall into one of two categories; the holidaymaking tourist and the island enthusiast. The tourist seeking a sun-soaked holiday in an exotic surrounding is usually attracted to the coast, with its ideal climate, excellent bathing and picturesque setting. The island enthusiast, on the other hand, comes as an explorer, wishing to get to know the island and its people, and perhaps to indulge in personal hobbies and interests.

For the tourist

If the coastal resort is the main tourist attraction, the occasional excursion makes a welcome distraction. From all the main resorts pleasant excursions can be made on foot and by public transport, while the most remarkable scenery can be seen on organised excursions of one or several days. From Ajaccio, Bastia and Calvi short walks into the hills behind the towns lead one to magnificent panoramas. The nearby villages are easily reached on foot and reveal the profusion of the natural plant life as well as the bewildering variety of crops. From Ajaccio visits can be made by both road and boat to the Iles Sanguinaires. Alternatively the southern borders of the Gulf of Ajaccio offer a panoramic circuit along the coast to Porticcio and Chiavari and an inland return route via the Col d'Aja Bastiano. The railway gives an opportunity to the individualist to pass a day in the superb mountains and forests around Vizzavona, or exploring the fortress town of Corte. A further excursion in the immediate vicinity of Ajaccio is to the Château de la Punta, stately home of the Pozzo di Borgo family. The château is set in large grounds commanding views both of the coast and inland to Monte d'Oro and Monte Renoso. A much longer excursion is to the Calanques de Piana, near Porto. There the red granite cliffs falling abruptly several hundred feet to the sea may be regarded as the most awe-inspiring spectacle in the island.

Calvi is equally well placed for short excursions. By boat the Grotto of the Veaux Marins can be visited in half a day while the day excursion from Calvi to Porto via the Golfe de Girolata is the finest sea excursion in the island. Excursions inland include the Cirque de Bonifato and the circuit of the Balagne via Muro, Belgodere, l'Ile-Rousse and Algajola. The independent traveller can make the short bus journey to Calenzana which is within four hours' walking distance of the summit of Monte Grosso, one of the best viewpoints. Alternatively, rail and bus routes link Calvi with l'Ile-Rousse, permitting exploration of the coast.

From both Bastia and St Florent, the essential excursion is the tour of Cap Corse, one of the island's showpieces. Bastia is also the starting point for the circuit of the Castagniccia, via the Golo valley, Ponte-Leccia, Morosaglia and Piedicroce, combining mountain scenery and traditional villages. As at Ajaccio, the railway permits a day excursion to Corte, while public bus services bring the pleasant *marine* villages between Bastia and Erbalunga within easy reach. In the south of Corsica, Porto-Vecchio, Propriano and Bonifacio are surrounded by open country which may be explored on foot and by public transport. From Porto-Vecchio, the circuit through the Forest of Ospedale to Zonza and via the Col de Bavella to Solenzara is considered to be perhaps the most beautiful itinerary in Corsica. Propriano is admirably situated for an exploration of the shores of the Gulf of Valinco, one of the largest and most deserted gulfs of the island. Excursions can also be made to the prehistoric monuments of Filitosa and the Rizzanese valley, while Sartène is less than ten miles inland. Bonifacio offers visits by boat to the sea grottoes of the limestone cliffs and to the off-shore islands of Lavezzi, San Bainzo and Cavallo. A twice-daily boat service to Sardinia permits a day visit to Santa Teresa, Palau or La Maddalena. Santa Teresa and Palau are small port villages, but La Maddalena is a town of over 11,000 inhabitants, formerly a naval base but now a small resort.

This list of excursions is by no means exhaustive and includes examples of those which may be made simply and inexpensively in the course of a day from established resorts. Longer excursions of several days, including all the major attractions of the coast and interior operate regularly throughout the summer.

For the island enthusiast

For many visitors, brief glimpses of the island will not satisfy the urge to explore or the will to pursue specialised interests. For these enthusiasts, as opposed to tourists, the attraction of Corsica is the opportunity to escape from the crowds and yet retain good weather and magnificent scenery.

The best way to savour the real Corsica is undoubtedly on foot and by such local transport as is available and convenient. Corsica offers ideal terrain for the sturdy walker for all the major summits are easily scaled although local consultation as to the choice of route and state of the weather is often desirable. The chief satisfaction of walking and climbing, apart from the scenery

189

and wildlife, is the encounter with the authentic Corsica and its inhabitants, the villagers and shepherds. The Niolo is perhaps the supreme area for mountain walking because of the ease of approach by road and rail, the concentration of major summits, and the persistence of traditional pastoral life. In fact almost the whole of the interior, and in particular the great forests, is excellent hiking and camping terrain.

The best centres for hiking and climbing are Asco, Calacuccia, Vizzavona, Bastelica and Corte, all of which give access to the island's highest peaks in the Niolo and adjacent ranges. From these centres, tracks traverse the maquis and forest to the open grasslands of the summits. Up there in summer, the foresters and shepherds may be the only human contact; they are invariably hospitable and helpful. Each centre has its particular attraction. Asco has an almost alpine character, reinforced by its recent development as a ski resort. Calacuccia has a central location from which to explore the entire Niolo, and Corte is the best starting point for the Restonica and Tavignano gorges. Vizzavona and Bastelica are summer mountain resorts with a rich variety of excursions from easy forest walks to the exploration of deep ravines and the ascent of major peaks. Asco and Calacuccia are centres of alpinism, but this should not be practised without expert guidance as the rock faces are difficult and dangerous for the uninitiated. The hardened walker will be tempted to walk from one to another of these mountain settlements, and this can be accomplished using only tracks that are totally undisturbed by noise, traffic or commercial manifestations. All the highest peaks can be ascended on foot without risk and are strenuous rather than difficult. Camping is the ideal formula as it permits impromptu variations in itinerary and penetration of areas remote from tourist influence.

For the less robust hiker, less tolerant of the summer heat and the occasional encounter with impenetrable maquis, an equally rewarding alternative to the peaks is to follow the valleys. Partticularly outstanding is the Porto valley, offering remarkable scenery in the Spelunca, the Forest of Aitone and the coast of

190

the Gulf of Porto. Porto and Evisa are good centres while the Col de Vergio gives access to the upper Golo valley where Calacuccia is a good centre to explore the Scala de Santa Regina gorges.

The enthusiast wishing to indulge personal interests may experience more difficulty than the hiker, for with the exception of natural phenomena, such as vegetation and wildlife, the principal features of interest are often scattered and Corsica is a large island. The archaeologist, for example, would first and foremost wish to visit Filitosa, followed by Aleria, and Mariana, as well as museums in Bastia, Corte and Ajaccio. This involves an itinerary of over 240 kilometres and includes diversions off the main roads. Similarly to see the finest Pisan churches or Genoese military architecture requires a careful choice of itinerary. The solution to this problem lies in careful planning, getting as much prior advice from appropriate authorities and societies as possible. Since much of the enjoyment of a holiday is to be found in its anticipation, the task of collecting information and of poring over a map is not an imposition to the true enthusiast.

POSTSCRIPT

This book has not been written as a guide to Corsica, or as a eulogy of its beauty. It attempts no more than to introduce the reader to the island and its people by setting them in the context of the geography, history and way of life. It has tried to balance the undoubted attractiveness of the landscape and the people against the equally undeniable difficulties which have dogged the island throughout history and which still exist. In the attempt to portray the island in this broad perspective, scant justice has been done to any one aspect. In particular the early history of the island is still imperfectly charted and the highly involved social and economic history of the middle ages and of the Genoese period is worthy of a lengthy book in itself. The complexity of the Corsican temperament, conditioned by a bitter history and a difficult present-day situation, defies easy analysis by an outsider.

191

ISLAND COMPENDIUM

The books in English by Dorothy Carrington, Geoffrey Wagner and Joseph Chiari are particularly vivid and spring from a profound understanding of the island. This book is, then, a humble prologue, and the reader is encouraged to read on, or better still, to go and see for himself.

APPENDIX A

CHRONOLOGY OF IMPORTANT EVENTS

565 BC	Alalia founded by Phocaeans
260–163 BC	Roman conquest
Fourth Century	Christianisation completed
Fifth–Sixth Centuries	Barbarian invasions
Sixth–Seventh Centuries	Byzantine occupation
Eighth–Tenth Centuries	Frequent Saracen incursions
1077	Pope Gregory VII cedes Corsica to the Bishop of Pisa
1133	Pope Innocent II divides Corsica between Pisa and Genoa
1284	Genoa defeats Pisa in naval battle of Meloria
1296	Pope Boniface VIII bestows Corsica and Sardinia on Aragon
1306	Death of Sinucello della Rocca, Giudice de Cinarca, in Genoese prison
1347	Defeat of Aragon; Genoese masters of the island
1358	Revolt led by Sambuccio d'Alando; creation of the *Terre des Communes*
1378	Arrigo de la Rocca attempts reconquest for Aragon; Genoa cedes control to a financial company, the *Maona*
1407	Vincentello d'Istria attempts reconquest for Aragon
1453	Genoa cedes control to the Bank of St George
1553	Sampiero Corso leads revolt against Genoa, aided by French troops under Maréchal de Thermes
1559	Treaty of Cateau-Cambrésis; Corsica returned to Genoa

1567	Death of Sampiero Corso in Genoese ambush
1571	Publication of *Statuti Civili e Criminali*
1676	Seven hundred Greek refugees installed at Sagone
1729	Revolt begins War of Independence
1731	Emperior of Austria sends troops in support of Genoa
1736	Arrival, coronation, and departure of Théodore de Neuhoff
1739–41	French military intervention and withdrawal
1747	Second French intervention under de Cursay in alliance with patriot Gaffori
1753	de Cursay interned by Genoese, Gaffori murdered
1755–69	Independence proclaimed with Paoli as General; Constitution published, university created at Corte, l'Ile-Rousse founded
1768	Treaty of Versailles; Genoa cedes Corsica to France
1769	Battle of Ponte Nuovo; Paoli, defeated, seeks refuge in London; Napoleon Bonaparte born at Ajaccio
1789	Corsica annexed to France
1790	Paoli returns to Corsica as Lieutenant-General
1793	Failure of Corsican expedition against Sardinia; Paoli impeached
1794–96	British intervention, Anglo-Corsican Kingdom
1796	British withdrawal, Paoli returns to London
1801	Miot Laws regulating customs and taxation
1807	Death of Paoli in exile
1838	Blanqui Report on the state of the Corsican economy
1922–40	Italian irredentist propaganda
1942	Italian landing and occupation in November
1943	Fall of Italy, general uprising, in September
1943	Battle of Bastia, in October; Corsica liberated
1957	Regional Plan published
1958	Reaction to Algerian Revolt; Committee of Public Safety formed
1969	Bicentenary celebrations of Napoleon's birth

APPENDIX B

PRINCIPAL FEAST DAYS

18 March	Ajaccio, Our Lady of Mercy, Patroness of the town
19 March	Bastia, St Joseph
Holy Thursday	Feast of the *canistrelli*, Calvi
Good Friday	*Cerca* and *granitola*, Erbalunga
	Processions of penitents, Calvi, Ajaccio, Bonifacio, Corte
	Procession of *Catenacciu*, Sartène
22 May	Feast of Ste Julie, Nonza
22 May	Greek Uniate celebration, Cargese
2 June	St Erasmus, festival of fishermen, Ajaccio
15 August	Feast of the Assumption
8 September	Pilgrimage, Our Lady of La Serra, Calvi
8–10 September	La Santa di Niolo, Casamaccioli
9 September	Pilgrimage, Our Lady of Lavasina
1 November	All Saints
8 December	Immaculate Conception
25 December	Christmas Day

FAIRS AND SECULAR FESTIVALS

1 January	New Year's Day, Public holiday
Shrove Tuesday	Carnival, Corte
Mid-Lent	Carnival, Ajaccio
12 May	Fair of St Pancras, Ajaccio
17 May	Fair of St Pascal, Corte
14 July	National feast day, Public holiday

APPENDIX B

1–15 August	Festival of Dramatic Art, Ajaccio
15 August	Celebration of Napoleon's birth, Ajaccio
	Festival, Calvi
8–10 September	Fair of Niolo, Casamaccioli
September	Trade Fair, l'Ile-Rousse
1–15 November	Tour of Corsica motor race

APPENDIX C

CLIMATIC TABLE

Month	Sunshine (hours)	Rainfall (mm)	Temperature range (°C)
January	119	70	0–17·7
February	138	72	−0·5–17·7
March	166	60	2·2–21·6
April	200	54	5·0–23·8
May	230	50	7·7–27·2
June	300	15	11·6–32·2
July	363	11	15·0–34·4
August	333	13	16·1–34·4
September	239	47	12·2–30·5
October	194	94	8·8–27·2
November	108	107	5·5–22·7
December	101	102	2·7–19·4

APPENDIX D

PRINCIPAL MONUMENTS AND HISTORIC BUILDINGS

PREHISTORIC SITES

Dolmens of Fontanaccia and Cauria, near Sartène
Menhir of Campomoro, near Propriano
Menhirs of Rizzanese
Camps at Filitosa (near Propriano), Castellu de Cucuruzzu (20km north-east of Sartène) and Torres (near Porto-Vecchio)

EXCAVATED ROMAN SITES

Aleria
Mariana

EARLY PISAN CHURCHES

La Canonica, Mariana
Cathedral of Nebbio, near St Florent
St Michel, Murato
Ste Christine, Cervione
Santo Pietro di Tenda
La Trinité, Aregno

BAROQUE CHURCHES

Ste Marie, St Jean-Baptiste, Bastia
Cathedral of Ajaccio
St Jean-Baptiste, Calvi

CONVENTS SCENE OF IMPORTANT CONSULTES

Orezza (ruins) : consultes of Terre des Communes and Rebellion
Alesani : coronation of Théodore de Neuhoff
Sant' Antonia della Casabianca : Paoli proclaimed General of Corsica

MUSEUMS

Archaeological Museum, Aleria
Repository of Roman excavation, Mariana
Museum of Corsican Ethnography, Bastia
Museum of Corsican History, Corte
Musée Napoléonien, Ajaccio
Musée Fesch, Ajaccio

HISTORIC BUILDINGS

Maison Bonaparte, Ajaccio
Chapelle Impériale, Ajaccio
Paoli's house, Morosaglia
Gaffori's house, Corte
Sampiero's house, Bastelica
Château de la Punta, family seat of Pozza di Borgo
Palais National, Corte, seat of Paoli's government
Tour de Capitello, battle site

MILITARY ARCHITECTURE

Genoese citadelles : Calvi, St Florent, Bastia, Porto-Vecchio, Bonifacio, Ajaccio
Corsican citadelles : Corte, Sartène
Genoese fortresses : Algajola, Girolata, Porto-Vecchio, Matra (Aleria), San Fiorenzo
Genoese bridges : Ponte-Leccia, Castirla, Pianella, Arbellara, Spelunca
Watchtowers : among the best preserved are Meria, Sagone, Porto, Erbalunga, Losse, Capitello, Miomo, Nonza, Pino, Rogliano, Olivo, Sisco, l'Isolella, Giraglia, Tollari, Centuri, Castellucio, Albo, Parajola Piani, Caldano, Gargalo, Parata, Capo di Muro, Porto-Pollo, Campo Moro, Olmeto, Santa-Manza, Diana, Alistro

BIBLIOGRAPHY

BOOKS

ALBITRECCIA, A. *La Corse*. Paris, 1933

ALBITRECCIA, A. *La Corse dans l'Histoire*. Paris, 1939

ALLORGE, P., ed. *Histoire du Peuplement de la Corse. Etude Bio-géographique*. Paris, 1926

AMBROSI, A. *Histoire des Corses et de leur Civilisation*. Bastia, 1914

ARCHER, D. *Corsica, the Scented Isle*. London, 1924

ARRIGHI, PAUL. *Histoire de la Corse*. Paris, 1969

AUDIBERT, R. and MORACCHINI, G. *La Corse*. Paris, 1955

BARRY, J. *Studies in Corsica*. London, 1893

BOSWELL, J. *An account of Corsica and Journal of a Tour in Corsica and Memoirs of Pasquale Paoli*. London, 1768

BOTTIGLIONI, G. *Atlante Linquistico Etnografico Italiano della Corsica*. Pisa, 1935

BOUCHARD, JEAN. *Flore Pratique de la Corse*. Bastia, 1964

CARLOTTI, J. *Monographie Agricole de la Corse*. Ajaccio, 1936

CARRINGTON, DOROTHY. *This Corsica*. London, 1962

CHIARI, JOSEPH. *Corsica. Columbus's Isle*. London, 1960

DAUDET, A. *Lettres de mon Moulin*. Paris, 1869

DECAUX, A. *Napoleon's Mother*. London, 1962

DUMAS, ALEXANDRE. *Les Frères Corses*. Brussels, 1844

FAUCHER, D., ed. *La France, Géographie Tourisme*, Vol 1. Paris, 1951

FLAUBERT, G. *Par les Champs et par les Grèves*. Paris, 1885

FORTESCUE, B. *Napoleon's Heritage*. London, 1924

GAI, DOM JEAN-BAPTISTE. *La Tragique Histoire des Corses*. Paris, 1951

GIACOBBI, F. *La Corse*. Paris, 1961

GIOVONI, C. *La Corse*. Paris, 1962

201

BIBLIOGRAPHY

GROSJEAN, ROGER. *Filitosa et son Contexte Archéologique*. Paris, 1961

GUELFI, J. *Visages de la Corse*. 2nd edition, Paris, 1967

HIGHHAM, ROGER. *Island Road to Africa*. London, 1968

HOUSTON, J. *The Western Mediterranean World*. London, 1964

KELLER, G. *Vignobles et vins de Corse*. Ajaccio, 1960

KOLODNY, Y. *La Géographie Urbaine de la Corse*. Paris, 1962

LARTILLEUX, H. *Géographie des Chemins de fer français, Volume 2, Réseaux Divers*. Paris, 1948

LES GUIDES BLEUS, *Corse*. Paris, 1965

MARTINI, MARIEN. *Le Cap Corse*. Bastia, 1960

MARTINI, MARIEN. *Les Corses dans l'Expansion Française*. Bastia, 1953

MASSIGNON, GENEVIEVE. *Contes Corses*. Gap, 1965

MERIMEE, PROSPER. *Notes d'un Voyage en Corse*. Paris, 1840

MERIMEE, PROSPER. *Mateo Falcone,* 1829

MERIMEE, PROSPER. *Columba*. 1841

MOREL, P. *La Corse*. Paris, 1969

NATALI, J. *La Poésie Dialectale Primitive du Peuple Corse*. Bastia, 1961

NAVAL INTELLIGENCE DIVISION. *Geographical Handbook Series, Corsica*. London, 1942

PIRIE, V. *His Majesty of Corsica*. London, 1939

PREFECTURE DE LA CORSE. *La Corse en quelques Chiffres*. Ajaccio, 1968

RONDEAU, A. *La Corse*. Paris, 1964

THOMPSON, I. B. *Modern France. A Social and Economic Geography* : Chapter 33, Corsica. London, 1970

THRASHER, P. *Pasquale Paoli: An Enlightened Hero 1725–1807*. London, 1970

UNESCO. *Report on Land Use in Semi-arid Mediterranean Climates: L'Utilisation du sol en Corse: Sur la Décadence d'un Terroir Insulaire*. Paris, 1962

VILLIEN-ROSSIE, M. L. *Petite Géographie du Département de la Corse*. Paris 1949

VILLAT, L. and others. *Visages de la Corse*. Paris, 1951

WAGNER, GEOFFREY. *Elegy for Corsica*. London, 1968

WAGNER, GEOFFREY. *Your Guide to Corsica*. London, 1960

BIBLIOGRAPHY

OTHER PUBLICATIONS AND PERIODICALS

BULLETIN DE LA SOCIETE DES SCIENCES HISTORIQUES ET NATURELLES DE LA CORSE. Bastia, since 1961

BULLETIN DE SOMIVAC SETCO. Bastia, since 1957

CORSE HISTORIQUE, ARCHEOLOGIQUE, LITTERAIRE, SCIENTIFIQUE (formerly *Revue D'Études Corses*). Ajaccio, since 1961

CORSICA VIVA. Paris, since 1963

ECONOMIC GEOGRAPHY. *Tourists in Corsica* by G. W. S. Robinson. Clark University, USA, 1957

GEOGRAPHICAL MAGAZINE. *The Revival of Corsica. Regional Planning in Action* by Ian Thompson. London, 1966

GEOGRAPHICAL MAGAZINE. *Trebizond to Corsica. The Story of an Imperial Migration* by Dorothy Carrington. London, 1956

GEOGRAPHY. *Land Reclamation in Eastern Corsica* by I. B. Thompson. London, 1962.

JOURNAL OF HELLENIC STUDIES. *Vitylo and Cargese* by H. Tozer, 1881

LA REVUE DE LA CORSE. Paris, 1920–39

LAND RECLAMATION IN THE SEVENTIES. *Land Reclamation in Eastern Corsica* by I. B. Thompson. Edinburgh, 1967

MEDITERRANEE. *La Population des Iles en Méditerranée* by Y. Kolodny. Aix, 1966

REVUE DE GEOGRAPHIE ALPINE. *Cargese—Essai sur la Géographie Humaine d'un Village Corse* by J. Coppolani. Grenoble, 1949

REVUE DE GEOGRAPHIE ALPINE. *Impressions Pastorales Corses* by C. Gardelle. Grenoble, 1970

REVUE DE GEOGRAPHIE ALPINE. *Notes sur la Maison Corse* by P. Mejean. Grenoble, 1932

REVUE DE GEOGRAPHIE ALPINE. *La Population de la Corse* by P. Lefebvre. Grenoble, 1957

REVUE DE GEOGRAPHIE DE LYON. *Tentatives de Mise en Valeur Agricole en Corse* by Janine Renucci. Lyon, 1961

REVUE DE GEOGRAPHIE DE LYON. *La Corse et le Tourisme* by Janine Renucci. Lyon, 1962

REVUE DE GEOGRAPHIE DE LYON. *Problèmes d'Aménagement de la Plaine Orientale en Corse* by Janine Renucci. Lyon, 1964

REVUE D'ETUDES CORSES. Ajaccio, 1954–60

BIBLIOGRAPHY

SCOTTISH GEOGRAPHICAL MAGAZINE. *Some Problems of Regional Planning in Predominantly Rural Environments. The French Experience in Corsica* by I. B. Thompson. Edinburgh, 1966

TRANSACTIONS OF THE INSTITUTE OF BRITISH GEOGRAPHERS. *Economy, Landscape and Society in la Castagniccia (Corsica) since the late Eighteenth Century* by P. Perry. London, 1967

U MUNTESE. In Corsican, Bastia (daily)

YALE REVIEW. *The Island that does not want to die* by Geoffrey Wagner. Yale University, USA, 1961

MAPS

The most useful and up-to-date topographical map is the *Carte Topographique*, 1 : 100,000, Corse, 8 sheets, 1966–7

Other topographical maps are 1 : 200,000, 2 sheets, 1943–44 and 1 : 50,000, 25 sheets, based on a survey of 1869–79

Geology : *Carte Géologique*, 1 : 80,000, 9 sheets, published in the 1890s

Vegetation : *Carte de la Végétation de la France*, number 80–81, 1 sheet, 1 : 200,000, Centre National de la Recherche Scientifique, Toulouse, 1963, with an accompanying handbook.

Tourist map : *Carte Michelin*, sheet 90, Corse, 1 : 200,000

ACKNOWLEDGEMENTS

This book is based on information and impressions gained during numerous visits to Corsica spanning a decade. I have visited the island as a tourist, a researcher and as a leader of a field expedition, and in each of these capacities received abundant kindness from both private individuals and officials. I would like especially to express my gratitude to Monsieur P. A. Carlotti, of the SOMIVAC AND SETCO development agency at Bastia. My appreciation of the island and its problems has been greatly enhanced by his willingness to give of his time and expertise.

The manuscript was expertly typed by Angela Flint and the maps were drawn by the Cartographic Unit at Southampton University under the supervision of Alan Burn. I am indebted to the French Government Tourist Office and to the Institut Géographique National in Paris for permission to reproduce the photographs acknowledged to them on page 10. Photographs provided by Monsieur P. A. Carlotti are reproduced by permission of *The Geographical Magazine*.

Finally, I would like to express my gratitude to Marguerita Oughton for the skill with which she edited, and greatly improved, my original manuscript.

INDEX

INDEX

INDEX

INDEX